AF584173

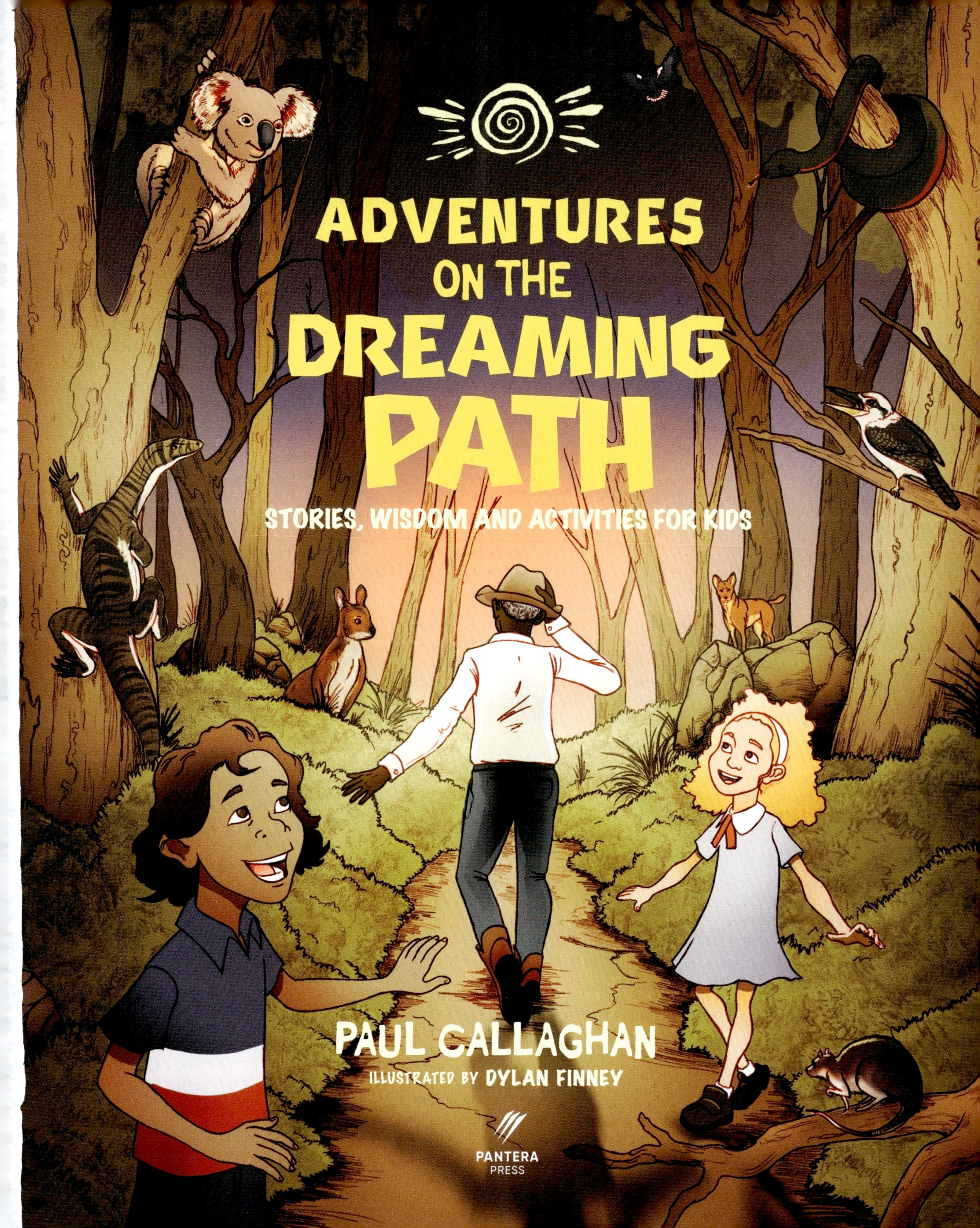
ADVENTURES
ON THE
DREAMING
PATH
STORIES, WISDOM AND ACTIVITIES FOR KIDS
PAUL CALLAGHAN
ILLUSTRATED BY DYLAN FINNEY
PANTERA
PRESS

To my mum.

Your love, your kindness and your caring
is a beacon for the world.

Although you left us far too soon,
I am thankful for being blessed
to be your son.

Nice
to meet
you!

HELLO, I'M UNCLE PAUL. Before I tell you about my book, it's important that I pay my respects to all Indigenous peoples around the world and Aboriginal Elders in Australia. I'm so happy you're here and would like to learn about my culture and hear some of our stories. It is my hope that once you read this book, you will want to find out more about Aboriginal culture where you live!

In our stories, our people say we have been living in this land now called Australia since the beginning of time. People who have lived on an area of land before anyone else and have a special connection with the land are sometimes called Aboriginal, Indigenous or First Nations people.

Through the stories in this book, you'll learn Aboriginal cultural and spiritual knowledge that is very special. What I share is based on what I have been taught, and it might be the same or different in other parts of Australia. Aboriginal people have been visiting each other and sharing stories and knowledge for tens of thousands of years. Although each nation and clan might have many things different, such as language, song, dance and story, we are also connected by our love for the land. In this book, you'll meet and get to know an Aboriginal Elder, Uncle Rolly, two children, Emily and Jacob, and the children's teacher, Ms Green. In each chapter, Uncle Rolly will tell you all a Dreamtime story, and afterwards, you'll join the four of them in having a yarn about it, just as if you were sitting around the fire together.

Sharing stories is a big part of Aboriginal culture. Stories give us time to slow down, bring us together, make us feel good and can also teach us things.

Together, we'll find the answers to some big questions.

An Aboriginal nation covers a distinct and large area of land. Within a nation, there are clan groups. Clans are larger than a normal family but are made up of people who are all related. Elders are people who have earned the respect of their clan for their wisdom, cultural knowledge and the good things they have done for others.

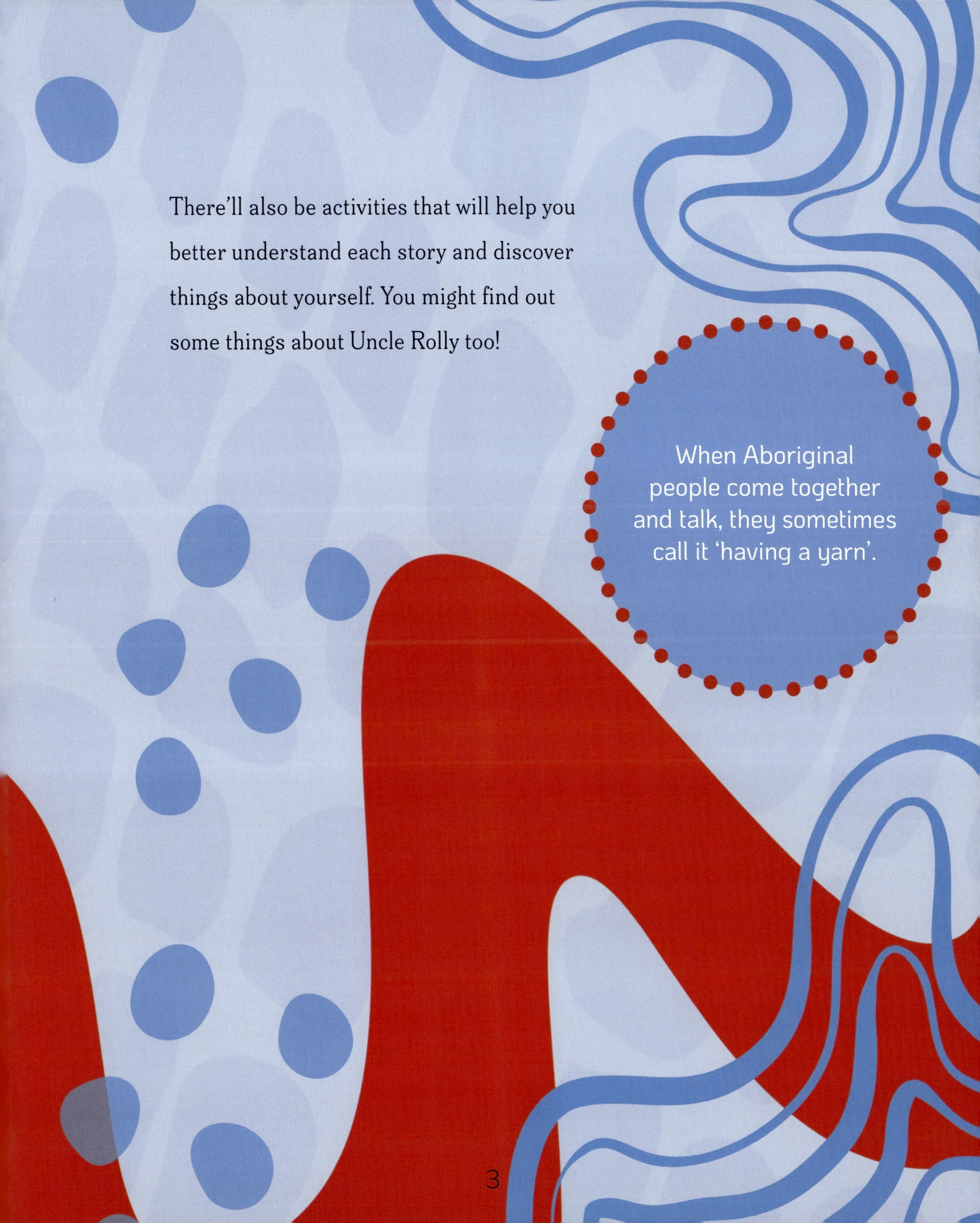

There'll also be activities that will help you better understand each story and discover things about yourself. You might find out some things about Uncle Rolly too!

When Aboriginal people come together and talk, they sometimes call it 'having a yarn'.

YOUR DREAMING PATH

For tens of thousands of years, as they grew, Aboriginal children were told lots of stories to help them understand the Dreaming Path. The Dreaming Path teaches us that the most important responsibility we will have in our life is to care for our place and all things in our place, including each other. How we do this is different for each person. We might be a teacher, or a mechanic or work in a shop, but no matter what we do, we always care for the land and everything that lives on it. When we talk about caring for our place, we are saying we must care for the land and the planet. We sometimes call the Earth our 'Mother', and she is the most beautiful thing that has ever existed.

As you explore the stories in this book, you'll realise how special you are, and how to connect with the land and live a happier life.

You will learn about

- the importance of story
- being yourself
- being different
- following your dreams
- friendship
- being healthy
- taking care of yourself
- loving and caring for Country
- sharing
- inspiration
- resilience
- happiness
- gratitude

When describing traditional Aboriginal stories, the word 'dream' makes them sound like fairytales, and not very useful for real life. But once you think about the meaning of these stories, you might better understand yourself and others and be able to live a happier life.

You might want to share these stories with friends, family and teachers – so you can talk about the messages they contain.

So, are you ready to meet Uncle Rolly and hear your first Dreamtime story?

CHAPTER 1

EMILY AND JACOB WERE waiting in the school library. Emily couldn't stop wriggling in her seat and running her fingers through her hair, which was starting to look like a dandelion puffball.

Jacob sat in his chair like a statue. Unlike Emily's, his hair was perfect.

'Aren't you excited?' Emily said, her eyes sparkling. 'I can't believe we're going to meet a real-life Aboriginal Elder.'

'Of course I'm excited.' Jacob blinked. 'I'm so nervous, I can't move.'

Milroy Primary School was large. It had so many students, and Emily and Jacob often felt unnoticed.

Ms Green's class was different. She made them feel special.

When Emily and Jacob had told Ms Green they would like to learn more about Aboriginal culture as their class project, Ms Green had arranged for Mr Ross, a local Elder, to come to the school.

There was movement outside and both children ran to the window.

Ms Green was strolling across the neatest of green lawns. With her was a small figure. The rolled sleeves of his light blue shirt glowed against his dark arms. Although he looked very old, he walked like a young man. Poor Ms Green was almost running to keep up with him.

Emily and Jacob hurried back to their seats as the library door opened. The man looked around the room for ages, shaking his head and smiling. His big bushy eyebrows failed to hide large brown eyes that didn't seem to blink. When he finally saw the children, he did a little jump as if he was surprised to see them.

'Who do we have here then?' he said. His brown eyes twinkled with mischief.

The children glanced at each other nervously.

'Hello, Mr Ross. I'm Emily.'

'Hello, Mr Ross. I'm Jacob.'

'Pleased to meet you both.' The old man removed a brown, worn-out cowboy hat as he spoke. The hat looked old – very old – as if it had seen many things and held many stories. 'First up, let's make a deal. If you call me Uncle Rolly, I'll feel a lot better.'

The children nodded. So did Ms Green.

Uncle Rolly paused and looked around the room. 'It's been so long since I've been in a school, let alone a library. Goodness. I've never seen so many books.' He scanned the room again, and his smile got even bigger.

‘So many stories,’ he said before sitting down. ‘Now, Ms Green and I have had a yarn about your project and agreed that I am going to catch up with you once a week for a couple of months. And after that, you’ll be doing a presentation to your class about what you’ve learned, ay?’

‘I’m pretty scared,’ Jacob said.

‘You’ll be right,’ Uncle Rolly replied. He smiled. ‘Do you know when I was your age, there were still dinosaurs around?’

‘Really?’ Jacob’s eyes were almost popping out of his head.

‘Yep. There’s even one named after me, Rollasaurus Rex.’

There was silence.

Then Uncle Rolly laughed so loud that Emily and Jacob jumped. ‘Naah. Just joking.’ He took a deep breath and his smile disappeared. ‘School has certainly changed though. When I was young, us kids weren’t allowed to go to a normal school. We had to go to a school where only Aboriginal children went.’

'You weren't allowed to go to a normal school?' Emily asked.

'We weren't allowed to do a lot of things other kids could do.'

There was sadness in Uncle Rolly's eyes. He gazed around the room and pointed to an Aboriginal artwork on the wall. 'Many people know about some of the beautiful things in our culture, but it's also important they know about some of the sad things that have happened to our people. My family lived on the outskirts of town, like all our people did, because no one wanted us in town or in their school. I never even met a non-Aboriginal person until I was a teenager.'

Emily gasped. There were students from over thirty different nations at Milroy Primary.

'As I grew up, I heard about shops, sporting grounds and a place where you could watch movies. It all sounded pretty exciting. One day, when we were fishing down by the river, I asked my mum when I could go into town. "Town sounds good," she told me, "but nothing can beat sitting here in Country." Then the fishing line she was holding started to tug and she pulled in a big perch. After she put that fulla in her bag, she looked at me and said, "We've got everything we need out here."'

Uncle Rolly clapped his hands together and sat upright. 'Now, I've done a lot of thinking about the best way to teach you about my culture and I think a good way might be by telling you a Dreamtime story each week. What do you think?'

Emily nodded in excitement, but Jacob looked sceptical.

'And after I tell you one of my Dreamtime stories, we're going to have a big yarn about it.' Uncle Rolly leaned forwards in his chair and whispered, 'So, are you ready for your first story?'

'Yes, please,' Emily said.

'Yes, please,' Jacob said unconvincingly.

And so, Uncle Rolly began.

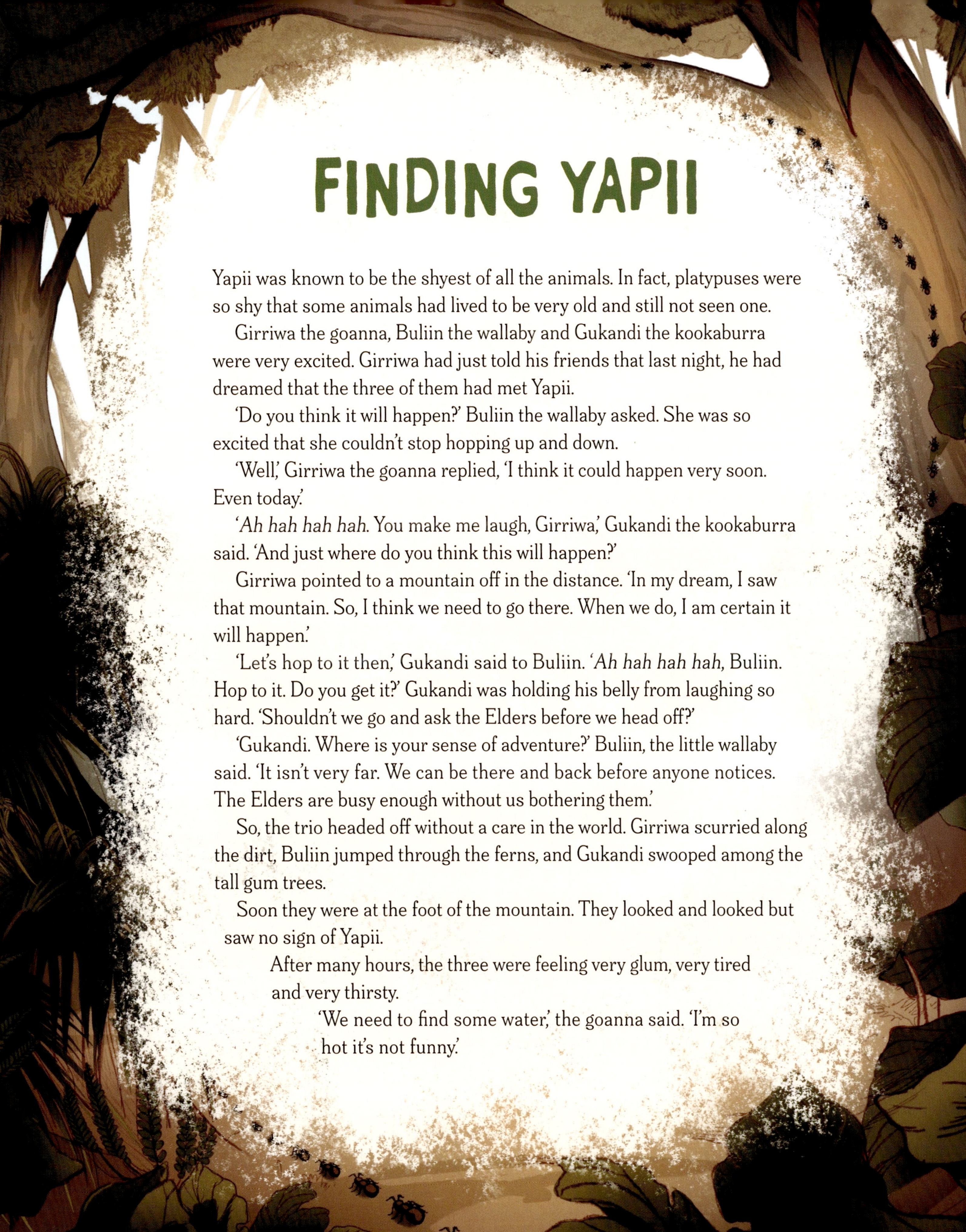

FINDING YAPII

Yapii was known to be the shyest of all the animals. In fact, platypuses were so shy that some animals had lived to be very old and still not seen one.

Girriwa the goanna, Buliin the wallaby and Gukandi the kookaburra were very excited. Girriwa had just told his friends that last night, he had dreamed that the three of them had met Yapii.

'Do you think it will happen?' Buliin the wallaby asked. She was so excited that she couldn't stop hopping up and down.

'Well,' Girriwa the goanna replied, 'I think it could happen very soon. Even today.'

'*Ah hah hah hah*. You make me laugh, Girriwa,' Gukandi the kookaburra said. 'And just where do you think this will happen?'

Girriwa pointed to a mountain off in the distance. 'In my dream, I saw that mountain. So, I think we need to go there. When we do, I am certain it will happen.'

'Let's hop to it then,' Gukandi said to Buliin. '*Ah hah hah hah*, Buliin. Hop to it. Do you get it?' Gukandi was holding his belly from laughing so hard. 'Shouldn't we go and ask the Elders before we head off?'

'Gukandi. Where is your sense of adventure?' Buliin, the little wallaby said. 'It isn't very far. We can be there and back before anyone notices. The Elders are busy enough without us bothering them.'

So, the trio headed off without a care in the world. Girriwa scurried along the dirt, Buliin jumped through the ferns, and Gukandi swooped among the tall gum trees.

Soon they were at the foot of the mountain. They looked and looked but saw no sign of Yapii.

After many hours, the three were feeling very glum, very tired and very thirsty.

'We need to find some water,' the goanna said. 'I'm so hot it's not funny.'

'You're right,' the kookaburra added. 'This isn't funny at all. I tell you what – I shall fly high into the sky. I'm sure I will see a stream or a pond.' Gukandi soared up through the trees and was back in the blink of an eye. 'There's a stream just over that small hill.' He pointed with his wing. 'It isn't very far at all.'

In no time, they were at the water's edge.

'The water looks so good, I'm going to get a run-up and jump right in,' Girriwa said.

'Please don't do that.' The voice was so faint that Girriwa, Buliin and Gukandi weren't sure they had heard anything at all. 'You might flood my home.'

'Where's that voice coming from?' Buliin sat up high on her tail and looked around. 'I can't see anybody.'

Girriwa thrust his long neck into the sky and looked very menacing. 'Who's there?' he said in his scariest voice.

A small furry animal appeared from behind a bush, looking nervous.

Girriwa lowered his head and tried to stay as still as possible so he didn't scare the little animal. He was so excited. 'You look the same as you did in my dream,' he said. 'We've come so far to see you, Yapii, and it's all worth it.'

'You are such a funny-looking animal.' Gukandi laughed. 'Just like the story says, you have the fur of a rat and the bill of duck. *Ah hah hah hah.* You must get very confused.'

'What do you mean?' the platypus replied.

'Well, which one are you? You can't be both.'

'I'm neither. I'm just me.'

'What do you mean?' The kookaburra scratched his head with his wing.

'I don't worry about trying to be anything. I just be me. When I was younger, I used to worry about being shy, until an Elder pointed out that I'm really good at listening.' Yapii laughed a tinkling kind of laugh that sounded like water gently crossing a rocky stream. 'Who would've thought that I have a superpower?'

The three friends became very animated.

'I wonder what my superpower is?' the goanna said.

'I think it's being a leader,' the wallaby replied.

'What do you think mine is?'

'That's easy,' the kookaburra said. 'You're always so positive. Now it's my turn.'

'It's your humour,' Buliin and Girriwa said at the same time.

'Ah hah hah hah.'

'Now I think about it,' Yapii said, 'your superpower is already inside of you. You find it by just being you.'

'Oh.' The kookaburra looked thoughtful.

Before long, the animals had made a new friend. Buliin, Girriwa and Yapii talked and talked, but Gukandi the kookaburra was unusually quiet. He hadn't even told a single joke.

Eventually Buliin the wallaby noticed. 'Is something wrong, Gukandi?'

'I have just been thinking about what Yapii said.'

'What did I say?' the platypus asked.

'You said "I'm just me". When you said it, you looked so sure of yourself. I know you are shy, Yapii, but you also seem to be very happy with who you are. Everyone sees me as the funny one, but sometimes I don't feel like that.'

'You don't have to be funny all the time.' Buliin leaned over and stroked Gukandi's feathers with her tail.

Gukandi nodded. 'Thank you, Buliin. From now on, I'm just going to be me. Sometimes I might be funny and sometimes I mightn't.'

'You have very good friends,' Yapii said.

The four shared stories for many hours, after which they sat quietly and watched the insects skating along the top of the water.

'I have had such a great time,' Yapii said. 'I hope you come back.'

'Speaking of time,' Buliin looked up to the sky, 'it's getting late. This has been the best day, Yapii, but we need to head home to our ngurra.'

Girrawa puffed up his chest with pride. 'I'm so glad we trusted my dream.'

After giving Yapii the biggest of hugs and promising they would return, the three friends scurried, hopped and flew home as fast as they could. They couldn't wait to share the story about the day they met Yapii.

HAVING A YARN

Uncle Rolly had been standing while he told the story. He now sat down, and Ms Green handed him a cup of tea. Uncle Rolly closed his eyes and made a slurping sound as he drank. Then there was quiet.

'Now,' he said in a loud voice. The children jumped, Ms Green jumped, and even the ants crawling outside the room jumped.

'When I was your age, me and the other kids didn't have fancy things like power or running water.' He chuckled. 'We didn't even get to eat meat or eggs much. But we didn't know any different. When we were allowed, us kids played in the bush and sometimes down by the river.'

He raised his cup in the air and smiled. 'And at night, the Old

People would tell us stories while they drank cups of tea.'

Emily pulled a face. 'I tried tea once. It was horrible.'

'Naah.' Uncle Rolly slowly lowered the cup to his lips again and made a slurping noise so loud that the librarian frowned in Ms Green's direction. 'It's beautiful.' He looked over to the librarian and winked. Ms Green's face went red. Then he turned back to the children. 'So, what did you think of the story? Did you learn anything?'

'I learned that platypuses are very shy animals and can be hard to find,' Jacob said.

'I learned how good it is to have friends, and to make new friends,' Emily added.

'That's very good,' Uncle Rolly said. 'The animals also realised that by being yourself, you can discover your special gifts ... your superpowers.'

'Does that mean I have a superpower?' Jacob asked.

'We all do,' Uncle Rolly replied. 'When I was a kid, the Old People would say to us, "You're made perfect, you know. If you look, listen and learn, you will grow into who you are meant to be and live a good life. Your story will be a good one."'

'How do you know if you're living a good life, Uncle?' Emily asked.

'When I was young,' he answered, 'I was taken to my first corroboree. I'd just got out of the car when one of my uncles spoke. "Stop for a second, nephew, and tell me what you notice," he said to me. I didn't notice anything to start with, but then I understood. "Uncle," I said, "the sky is full of laughter." I've never forgotten that lesson.'

'So, living a good story is about laughing a lot?' Jacob asked.

'Yes and no,' Uncle Rolly replied. 'Aboriginal people laugh a lot. Even when life is hard, our people focus on the good things, rather than the things they don't have. Living a good story is about believing in yourself and not trying to be someone you aren't.'

Ms Green looked at her watch and then at Uncle Rolly. 'I'm afraid that's it for today.'

A groan filled the room.

Uncle Rolly chuckled. 'Don't worry, we'll have plenty of time to catch up, you fullas. But thanks for yarning with me today. It's been lovely.'

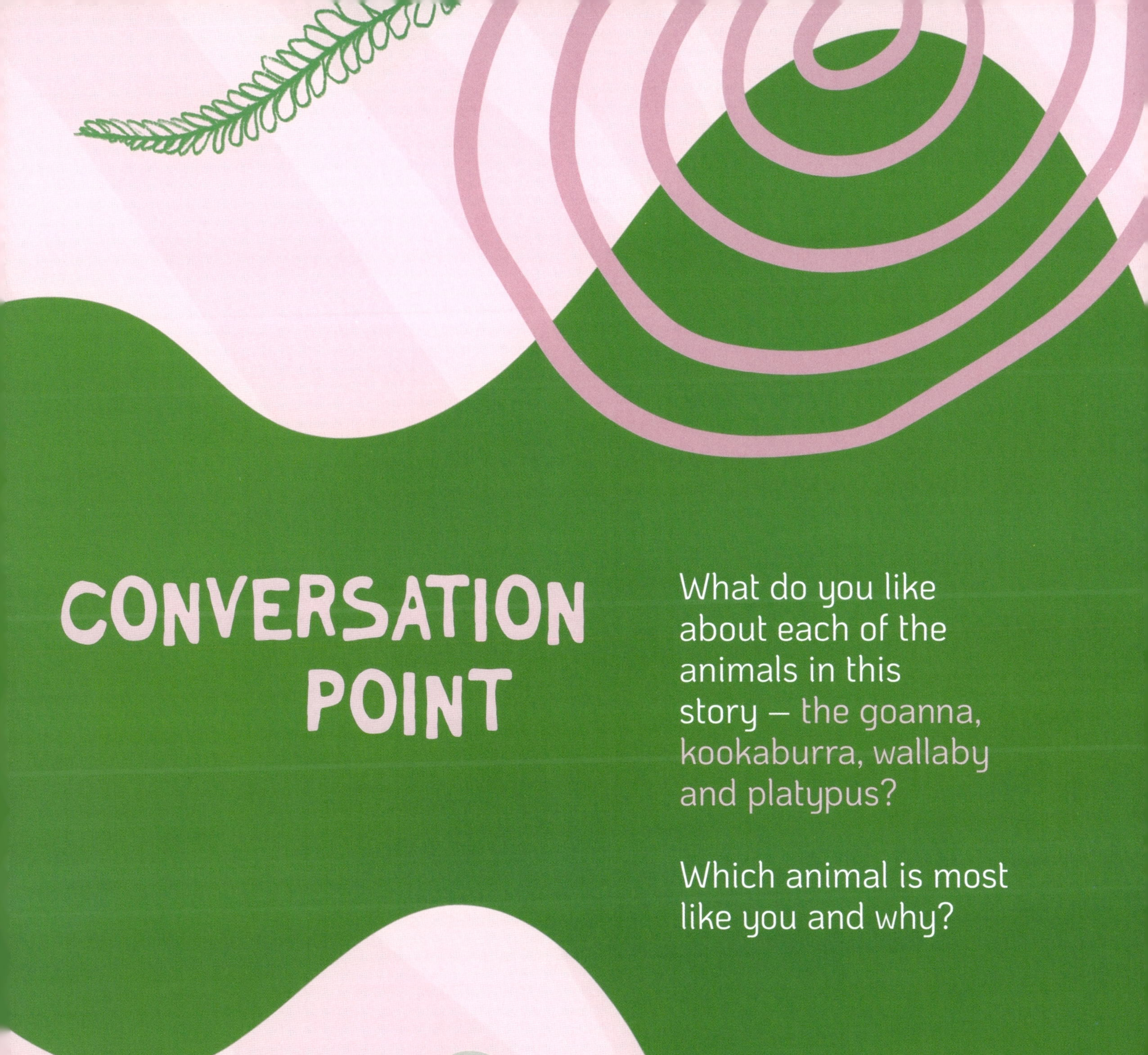

CONVERSATION POINT

What do you like about each of the animals in this story – the goanna, kookaburra, wallaby and platypus?

Which animal is most like you and why?

ACTIVITY

Feeling Special

The story of Yapii tells us about friendship, and how good friends like us the way we are. When you walk in the bush, everything you can see is special – just like you are!

THINGS YOU WILL NEED:

- Coloured pencils, crayons or markers
- A blank piece of paper.

1. On a blank piece of paper, draw a large tree with lots of branches. Make sure there's plenty of space above the tree for the sky. Also, make sure the branches are far enough apart from each other to draw bubbles in which you can write words.
2. Draw six large bubbles hanging from the branches of your tree.
3. In each of the bubbles, write something special about yourself.
4. Under your drawing, write a sentence about how special you are.

CHAPTER 2

DURING THE WEEK, Emily and Jacob had talked so much in Ms Green's class that she'd had to ask them to calm down. It was unusual to hear her use such a stern tone.

'But Ms Green, listening to Uncle Rolly is so interesting. And everything else is so boring,' Emily said.

The following day they heard Uncle Rolly's laughter echoing down the hallway. He entered the music room where they sat waiting and placed a cloth bag on the ground, before walking over to a guitar and picking it up.

'Good morning, you two.' He plucked each string until he was satisfied the instrument was in tune. His voice was soft, as was his strumming, yet the song was haunting and demanding of their attention. As he sang, his eyes became dreamy and distant.

When he finished, he placed the guitar back in its stand with great care. 'I learned to play when I was a teenager. We all did,' he said. 'That's how we entertained ourselves.'

'What was that song you just played?' Jacob asked. 'It sounded kind of sad.'

'It's a song about a mother's love,' Uncle Rolly replied. 'One of her children is taken away and she sits by the window every day and night hoping she will return. See, when we were kids, we'd be playing and if we saw dust in the distance, we knew a car was coming to take one or more of us kids away. So, that song is very special to me. But that song is also about hope.' He slapped a cymbal with an open hand. The ringing bounced off the walls and made everyone jump again. 'And that, ladies and gentlemen,' he said with a laugh, 'is the perfect way to introduce today's story.'

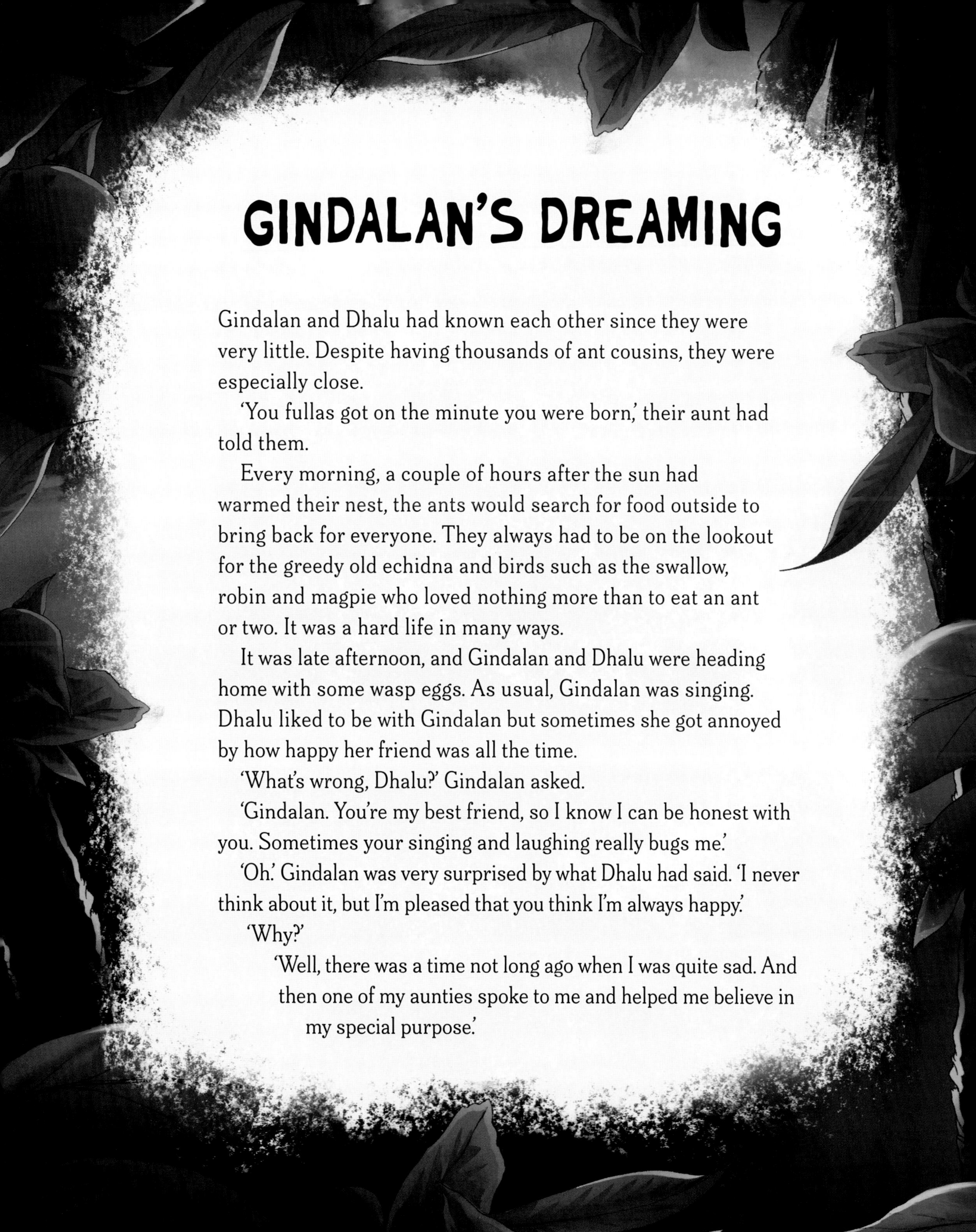

GINDALAN'S DREAMING

Gindalan and Dhalu had known each other since they were very little. Despite having thousands of ant cousins, they were especially close.

'You fullas got on the minute you were born,' their aunt had told them.

Every morning, a couple of hours after the sun had warmed their nest, the ants would search for food outside to bring back for everyone. They always had to be on the lookout for the greedy old echidna and birds such as the swallow, robin and magpie who loved nothing more than to eat an ant or two. It was a hard life in many ways.

It was late afternoon, and Gindalan and Dhalu were heading home with some wasp eggs. As usual, Gindalan was singing. Dhalu liked to be with Gindalan but sometimes she got annoyed by how happy her friend was all the time.

'What's wrong, Dhalu?' Gindalan asked.

'Gindalan. You're my best friend, so I know I can be honest with you. Sometimes your singing and laughing really bugs me.'

'Oh.' Gindalan was very surprised by what Dhalu had said. 'I never think about it, but I'm pleased that you think I'm always happy.'

'Why?'

'Well, there was a time not long ago when I was quite sad. And then one of my aunties spoke to me and helped me believe in my special purpose.'

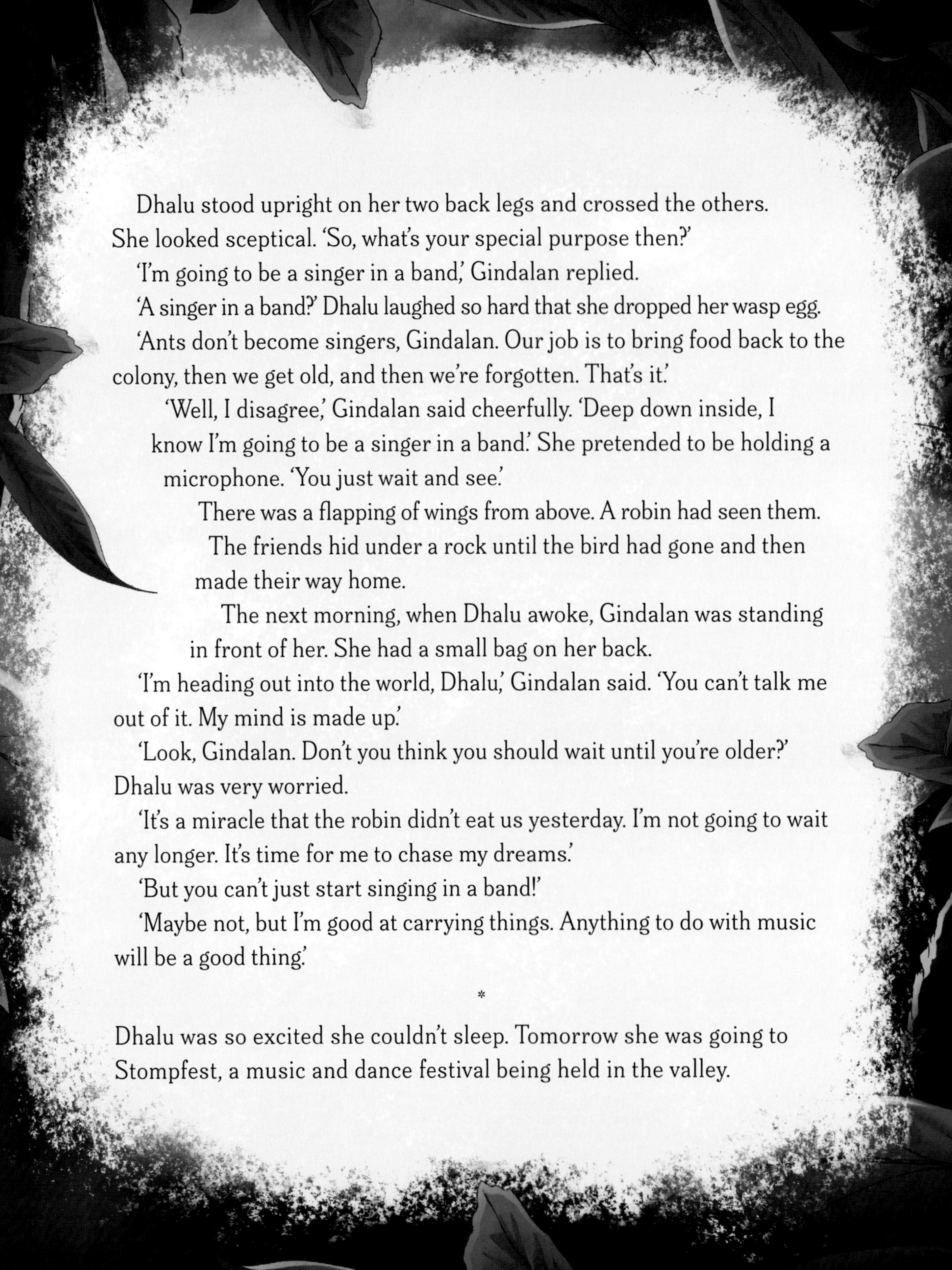

Dhalu stood upright on her two back legs and crossed the others. She looked sceptical. 'So, what's your special purpose then?'

'I'm going to be a singer in a band,' Gindalan replied.

'A singer in a band?' Dhalu laughed so hard that she dropped her wasp egg. 'Ants don't become singers, Gindalan. Our job is to bring food back to the colony, then we get old, and then we're forgotten. That's it.'

'Well, I disagree,' Gindalan said cheerfully. 'Deep down inside, I know I'm going to be a singer in a band.' She pretended to be holding a microphone. 'You just wait and see.'

There was a flapping of wings from above. A robin had seen them. The friends hid under a rock until the bird had gone and then made their way home.

The next morning, when Dhalu awoke, Gindalan was standing in front of her. She had a small bag on her back.

'I'm heading out into the world, Dhalu,' Gindalan said. 'You can't talk me out of it. My mind is made up.'

'Look, Gindalan. Don't you think you should wait until you're older?' Dhalu was very worried.

'It's a miracle that the robin didn't eat us yesterday. I'm not going to wait any longer. It's time for me to chase my dreams.'

'But you can't just start singing in a band!'

'Maybe not, but I'm good at carrying things. Anything to do with music will be a good thing.'

*

Dhalu was so excited she couldn't sleep. Tomorrow she was going to Stompfest, a music and dance festival being held in the valley.

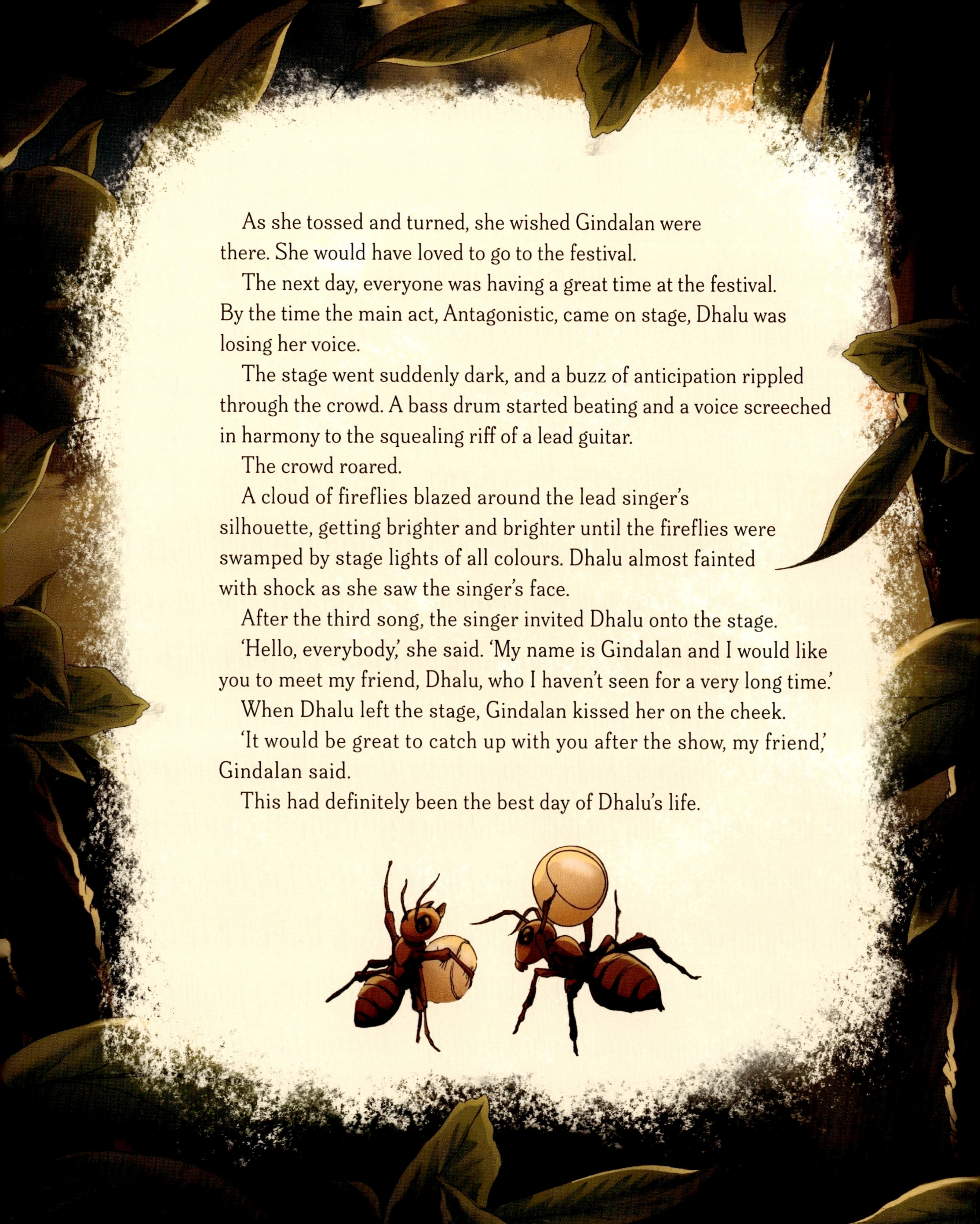

As she tossed and turned, she wished Gindalan were there. She would have loved to go to the festival.

The next day, everyone was having a great time at the festival. By the time the main act, Antagonistic, came on stage, Dhalu was losing her voice.

The stage went suddenly dark, and a buzz of anticipation rippled through the crowd. A bass drum started beating and a voice screeched in harmony to the squealing riff of a lead guitar.

The crowd roared.

A cloud of fireflies blazed around the lead singer's silhouette, getting brighter and brighter until the fireflies were swamped by stage lights of all colours. Dhalu almost fainted with shock as she saw the singer's face.

After the third song, the singer invited Dhalu onto the stage.

'Hello, everybody,' she said. 'My name is Gindalan and I would like you to meet my friend, Dhalu, who I haven't seen for a very long time.'

When Dhalu left the stage, Gindalan kissed her on the cheek.

'It would be great to catch up with you after the show, my friend,' Gindalan said.

This had definitely been the best day of Dhalu's life.

HAVING A YARN

After he finished telling the story, Uncle Rolly picked up the cloth bag and put his hand inside it. The bag was old, tattered and coated with drawings that looked as if they'd been done by children a long, long time ago. As the contents of the bag rattled and banged, a wonderful smell filled the room. Uncle Rolly pulled out a small branch that was cloaked in gum leaves. He closed his eyes and inhaled. 'Can't beat the smell of mother nature,' he said. 'It's all around us, and a lot of people don't even notice.'

The children closed their eyes and allowed the smell to consume them.

There was more rattling and banging. The children opened their eyes and giggled. Uncle Rolly's head was almost completely inside the bag.

'Where are you?' His voice was muffled. 'Aah. Got you.' He held up two pieces of dark, polished wood. They were rounded, about twenty centimetres long and two centimetres wide. 'These are called clapsticks,' he said.

'They're an important musical instrument for

Aboriginal people.' He looked around the room and grinned. 'Learn to play music, you fullas, and your life will be a much happier one.'

He struck the clapsticks together, and a crisp ring cut through the air. 'Here.' He passed the children and Ms Green a clump of gum leaves. 'As I sing this song, I want you to smell these leaves and think about nature.'

Uncle Rolly sang in a language the children had never heard before. His face looked old and young at the same time and joy filled the room.

The clapsticks clattered the gentlest of goodbyes as they were placed back in the bag.

'That song was about me walking Country and feeling the love that is all around me. You see, the trees, the animals, the rocks, everything in nature is family. We're all connected.'

Singing is very important to Aboriginal people. Each song tells a story that can help you live a good life. Each song also has a dance. Song, dance and story are connected, just like a family.

'Sometimes my dad takes me for walks in the national park,' Emily said. 'I love it.'

'I'd love to do that.' Jacob's face had lost its glow. 'But no-one in our family has a car and we just don't do that kind of stuff.'

'You never know,' Emily replied. 'One day it might happen.'

Jacob shrugged. 'Sometimes it's easier to give up.'

'Don't I know all about wanting to give up,' Ms Green said.

Both children looked at her. It was a shock to hear her speak, and an even bigger shock to hear her speak about giving up.

'When I was at high school,' she continued, 'I nearly left because of kids making fun of me. And I found university very hard at times as well.'

'But you're so clever, Ms Green.' Jacob looked astonished.

'I always dreamed of being a teacher. That kept me going, I guess.'

'That's the secret.' Uncle Rolly tapped the cymbal gently this time. It made the loveliest shimmering sound. 'It's important to have dreams and chase them, even when you're my age.'

'Can you tell us some of your dreams, Uncle?' Jacob said.

'Well, when I was your age, I dreamed of having shoes. Me and the others used to have to walk to school in bare feet, see. Summer was fine, ay, but winter wasn't so good. And when I was a bit older, I really wanted a new pair of jeans.' He looked down at the neatly ironed blue jeans he was wearing.

'I was in town and went into a milk bar for the first time.'

'What's a milk bar?' Jacob asked.

'It's like a cafe, ay,' Uncle Rolly replied. 'So, I went into the milk bar and a group of young people were standing by the jukebox dressed in the latest jeans. They looked real neat. One fulla yelled out, "Look at the blackfulla," and they all laughed. I ran home so fast I could have made the Olympics that day.'

'That would have been awful,' Ms Green said.

'It wasn't great, that's for sure. But when I was about sixteen, I started to learn more about my culture. And the more I learned, the more I realised that I didn't need those flash jeans or record player or the approval of others to be happy. So, these days I have one big dream, and that's for all people to be kind to one another, to care for each other and to care for the land as well. That's what our culture teaches us.'

'Wow,' Jacob said. 'That's a really big dream.'

'That's the good things about dreams. You can make them whatever you want them to be,' Uncle Rolly said. 'See. My parents didn't have a lot of money or a house or a car so they couldn't give me wealth, but they gave me love and culture. If my culture can help the world be a little bit better, than I can be happy with my story.'

Jacob scratched his nose as he thought about what Uncle Rolly had said.

Emily watched Jacob and started scratching her nose. When they both looked at Uncle Rolly, he was scratching his nose too, along with Ms Green.

'Nothing like scratching the old nose to get your mind thinking properly.' Uncle Rolly chuckled.

'My uncle told me that, when he was a kid, he dreamed of being a racing car driver, but he never became one,' Jacob said.

Uncle Rolly nodded. 'A lot of people don't follow their dreams. It might be because they had responsibilities that were more important. But sometimes it's because they're frightened of failing. It took me six years before I went back to that milk bar, but when I finally did, I didn't care who was watching me. And I finally had that caramel milkshake I had dreamed about.' He pretended to sip from a straw. 'And it was just lovely.'

'Did you wish you had done that sooner?' Emily asked.

'Nah. There was no rush. I did it just when I was meant to.' He put his imaginary milkshake on the floor. 'I've had many good times in my life, Emily. And I've had some pretty bad ones. But I wouldn't change any of it. They're all important parts of my story.'

'Dhalu seemed to be scared of a lot of things, didn't she?' Emily said after a while. 'While Gindalan didn't seem to be frightened at all.'

'Fear can warn us of danger, which is a good thing. But fear can also hold us back from walking our footsteps and following our Dreaming Path.' Uncle Rolly waved a finger in the air. 'Are you going to let that fear fulla boss you around? Or are you going to be the boss?'

'I think it's better to be the boss,' Jacob said. Emily nodded.

'Think about Dhalu and Gindalan,' Uncle Rolly said. 'To be frightened of that robin was very real. But if Gindalan had been too frightened to ever leave the nest again, she would never have made her dreams come true.'

'I'm sorry to interrupt, Uncle.' Ms Green looked a little bit nervous. 'But we're just about out of time.'

The sound of disappointment flooded the room.

Uncle Rolly smiled at the children. 'Never mind. We'll be catching up again next week. And even better, we're going somewhere that is very special to me. I'll give you a clue: it's out in the bush.'

Disappointment turned to excitement. Then he sprang out of his chair like a much younger person. 'Remember, you fullas, try to laugh as much as you can,' he said before skipping across the carpet to the door.

CONVERSATION POINT

Listed below are fears we might face as we get older.

- Not being liked
- Being laughed at
- Not fitting in
- People disagreeing with us
- Failure
- Being judged
- Disappointing someone
- Being seen as different

How can they hold you back from finding your Dreaming Path?

How do you make sure they don't stop you from being the *real* you?

ACTIVITY

Following Your Dreams

Dreams are what help us follow our Dreaming Path. The good thing about dreams is you can make them whatever you want them to be.

THINGS YOU WILL NEED:

- Coloured pencils, crayons or markers
- Drawing of tree from Chapter 1 activity.

1. On the drawing of your tree with bubbles, draw several large clouds in the sky.
2. In a cloud, write one of your dreams.
3. Do this in each cloud until you have run out of dreams to write about.

CHAPTER 3

UNCLE ROLLY WAS EXCITED. Meeting with the children each week had given him a spark in his heart that he hadn't expected. Although he always appreciated the positives in his life, the sadness would still grab him sometimes. When it did, he would find it hard to be his normal happy self. But not today. He had asked a nephew to take him to Big Rock Bend early, so he could prepare a campfire and have everything just right for the children.

Uncle Rolly lay back in his chair and waited, the warm sunlight trickling through the leaves of the river gums. He took a deep breath and sighed. He thought about the search he had started so many years ago. Patience had become his best friend after all those years. *It will be worth the wait,* he always reminded himself. He was brought back to the present by the sound of a car approaching.

Ms Green and the children climbed from the car, and

scrambled down the rocky slope with their fold-up chairs. Ms Green was dressed in jeans and running shoes, looking very un-teacher-like. Emily and Jacob were also out of uniform.

After everyone had said hello, they sat down and patiently waited for Uncle Rolly to speak. The fire crackled for what seemed a long time.

Uncle Rolly carefully positioned some wood on the fire, moving it several times before he was happy with it. 'Our Old People say, "When you want to sort out a problem, go bush. Just sit down and feel the magic that surrounds you. That's when you'll find peace."' The sweet warble of a magpie filled the air, and Uncle Rolly looked up to a tree nearby. 'I see you, my sister,' he said. 'And yes – we will make sure we enjoy this Country and not leave any mess behind.' He turned back to the children. 'Everything in the bush communicates, as you'll find out in this story.'

YUNARA UNDERSTANDS HIS PLACE

Yunara lived in saltwater country. Every day, he stood in the same place and watched the tide come in and go out. His uncles and aunties did the same thing. Some of them had been doing this for almost 100 years.

Although Yunara respected his Elders, he couldn't bear the thought of following in the footsteps of his aunties and uncles. When he told them he wanted to do other things, the Elders gently told him it wasn't possible. His cousins weren't so nice. Some even laughed at him.

Watching the tide come in and go out had its good points. Yunara always enjoyed seeing the fish swimming around his feet and the birds darting across the water.

But sometimes, Yunara wished he could be Dhunggaarr, the pelican, floating around like a cloud high up in the sky. I bet he sees so many interesting things, he would think. Yunara felt very unimportant.

'I've been watching you for a while now, Yunara,' his grandfather said. 'And you don't seem to be at peace. Is there anything you'd like to tell me?'

'Well, Grandfather,' Yunara said. 'I know how thankful I should be for everything I have, but I can't help thinking how boring my life is, and how unimportant I am.'

His grandfather didn't say anything.

'I don't want to sound ungrateful, Grandfather, but I look around and see

my cousins, uncles and aunties doing the same thing as me.' Yunara sighed sadly. 'I just think that if I wasn't here, no one would miss me. Sometimes, I wish I weren't a tree.'

It was quiet for a while and then the grandfather spoke.

'I can understand how you feel, Grandson. I felt like that too when I was your age.'

'Really?'

'Of course,' his grandfather replied. 'We are part of the Dilingiribang clan. Mangrove trees have been in this country since the beginning. We're everywhere up and down the coast. So, I understand how you might feel unimportant. When I was younger, and even now sometimes, I found myself imagining how it would feel to be a hawk speeding through the sky, or a kangaroo leaping through the bush. Their lives seem far more exciting than being stuck in the mud every day.'

'Exactly,' Yunara said. His voice sounded very far away as he imagined jumping through the bush like a kangaroo.

'There are things we can change in our life, Yunara, and there are things we can't.'

A breeze swept through the area, rustling the leaves of the many mangrove trees. 'Ahhh. That feels so good,' the old tree said. 'Yunara, you know I love you, but I need to remind you that this is who you are. So, you can choose to accept this and feel proud of who you are, or you can choose to get yourself down about it.'

'I know what you're saying, Grandfather, but what's so great about me?'

'Well, although we don't look as pretty as the kingfisher who sits in our branches, the Dilingiribang clan is very important. Without us, Mother Earth and her children will suffer.'

'How?' Yunara said.

'My old friend Gangalba the cormorant tells me we are the only tree in the world that can live in salt water. So, that makes us very special. And our roots are home for many fish. Without us, those little fullas would have nowhere to live.'

Yunara looked down at the small fish that surrounded him. He suddenly felt very protective of them. 'I had no idea,' he said.

'If our clan didn't exist, the coast would be washed away by storms, and the water would not be as clean.' The old tree smiled a happy mangrove-tree smile. 'You are more important than you will ever know. You see, the big story is made up of the little stories within it.' The wind started to blow stronger. 'Feel that wind?'

Yunara nodded, his branches and leaves making the most musical sound.

'That's the spirits telling you what I say is true. Without each of us, there is a gap in the story. Mother Earth cannot be well if all her children aren't well. Always remember how special you are.'

The wind was lighter now. There was quiet as Yunara and his grandfather enjoyed the breeze. Eventually the old mangrove spoke again.

'It's important to love who you are, Yunara, and not wish your life away by comparing yourself to others or wanting to be someone else. You've been created the way you are for a reason. As you grow, that reason will become clearer.'

'Thank you, Grandfather.' Yunara noticed a pod of dolphins passing by. He felt happy for them instead of feeling jealous. Our clan keeps the river healthy for you fullas, he thought. 'I love you,' Yunara said.

'I love you too,' his grandfather replied.

HAVING A YARN

As Uncle Rolly had told the story, a wind had picked up, and it got stronger and stronger, making the trees dance and groan. When he finished speaking, the wind stopped, as if a fan had been turned off.

'When we sit out in the bush, everything around us is listening,' Uncle Rolly said. The loud growl of a male koala ambushed their camp. Everyone jumped except Uncle Rolly, who sat as if nothing had happened. 'But there's no need to be frightened. The more you come out here and sit, the more you will learn about what you see, hear and smell. That old koala is just saying hello. The bush is happy when it hears people sharing stories about culture.'

There was quiet for a moment, then Emily spoke. 'In the story, the trees can think and speak. So, are you saying the bush is alive?'

'Yes I am.'

'The story is also telling us that everything is special, isn't it?' Jacob added.

'That's right,' Uncle Rolly replied. 'The world is very big, and it's very easy for a person to think they aren't important and their life is meaningless, just like Yunara did. That's why Yunara dreamed of being something else.'

'But life can be so boring, Uncle Rolly. Especially school.' Jacob threw a stone into the bush.

'Did you ask that stone if it was okay to take it from its home?'

Jacob looked at the ground. 'No.'

Uncle Rolly walked over to where the stone had landed. 'Now. Where's that giba hiding?' He returned with the stone and rested it gently in the dust. 'There you go, little fulla. Everything is good now.' The Elder sat in his chair. 'Now, where were we?'

'Wanting to be a pelican made Yunara unhappy, didn't it?' Emily said.

Uncle Rolly nodded.

A kookaburra started cackling. They all looked over to a gum tree, its bark a ripple of brown and cream, like marble chocolate.

'I hear you, Gukandi.' He looked back to the children. 'He's always laughing, that fulla.' He made a cackling noise similar to the kookaburra, and the bird responded. 'He's just come back from town and is laughing at all the people looking at their phones instead of the river. Now, Yunara's grandfather said he didn't want Yunara to wish his life away. What do you think he meant when he said that?'

'I think he was telling Yunara to think about all the good things he has instead of wanting things he can't have,' Emily said.

'Very good.' Uncle Rolly nodded. 'The trick to a good life is to flow like the river. You watch a leaf flowing downstream. It might get caught on something, but eventually the water will push it back out into the stream, and away it goes. People get caught up at red lights and get so impatient even though they know it's going to turn green at some point.' He started to laugh.

'I mean, why get angry at a set of traffic lights? The traffic lights don't care.' His laughter rang across the bush.

'Now, talking about going with the flow, why don't we go and explore this river?'

How do you think Yunara was feeling at the start of the story?

How do you think Yunara was feeling at the end of the story?

Why did you think the way he was feeling changed?

CONVERSATION POINT

ACTIVITY

The Canoe

Being patient is about being calm and waiting for things to happen, rather than getting upset and wishing they were happening right now. Aboriginal people have been going with the flow since the beginning of time.

THINGS YOU WILL NEED:

- You.

1. Find somewhere you can sit or lie down without anyone bothering you.
2. Take some deep breaths in and out.
3. When you're ready, imagine you're in a canoe in the middle of a freshwater stream. The water is flowing and so clear you can see the different coloured stones, and even some fish.
4. You're worrying about where the canoe ride will finish and then you realise it doesn't matter. In your mind, you're just going to enjoy the ride.
5. You paddle and float down the stream and can see the most beautiful birds, plants and trees. The sound of the water flowing is very soothing and you have never felt so happy.
6. Enjoy the ride for as long as you like and watch where the canoe takes you.
7. When you're ready, take some deep breaths and let the picture go.
8. How do you feel?

CHAPTER 4

'YES!' JACOB SAID excitedly, pumping his fist into the air. Emily did the same. Ms Green had just told them they were going to meet with Uncle Rolly out in the country again.

Ms Green was feeling a little bit anxious as she drove along the dusty, potholed track, not that Emily and Jacob noticed. They were too busy chatting away in the back seat.

Ms Green gave a relieved sigh when she saw Uncle Rolly up ahead. A plume of smoke from the campfire next to him seemed to reach out across the grassy clearing and welcome them. As the trio walked across the paddock, Ms Green noticed there were bricks and strands of wire scattered here and there like pieces of a jigsaw puzzle.

'This is where I grew up,' Uncle Rolly said. He stood up with his arms outstretched and turned around in a circle. 'The government made us move away from here a long time ago. Nothing here now but memories.' He smiled. 'I've got something special planned for today. We're going to be making Johnny cakes.'

Jacob and Emily had never heard of 'Johnny cakes'. They watched Uncle Rolly mix the flour, water and salt into a dough, which he then broke into balls the size of a scoop of ice cream.

'We used to live on these when I was little,' he said.

He flattened the balls and put them on a wire rack over some hot coals. A delicious smell rose into the air as they cooked. 'There you go.' He placed one Johnny cake each on three separate plates. 'To really enjoy them, slap on as much butter and golden syrup as you are game to.'

'These are the best things ever,' Jacob said. He licked the golden syrup and butter off his fingers and grinned. 'You were so lucky as kids to have these.'

'We were lucky all right,' Uncle Rolly said. 'But things weren't easy at times.' The wrinkles in the old man's face stood out more than usual. 'My father told me how our people were rounded up like cattle and made to live here. There was a big fence right around this place to lock us in.' He pointed to the strands of wire and several battered and worn

posts that circled the clearing. 'No one could leave the Reserve without the approval of the manager. We had no say in anything.'

'That's terrible,' Emily said.

'Yes. But our people still laughed every day.' The old man looked to the sky, and tears glistened on his cheeks. 'Except when the children were taken away.'

'Why were the children taken away?' Jacob said, his voice trembling.

'Well, not that long ago, the government had a law that allowed them to take Aboriginal children away because they thought it would give those kids a better life. But they were wrong. It created a lot of pain and suffering.' The old man collapsed into his chair and looked very old and tired. 'A lot of kids were taken and never saw their families again. I remember the day they took my sister. My mum and dad held us tight, but she got taken all the same.' His eyes were red. 'I was the last of my brothers and sisters left in my family. I still look for them when I'm travelling.' He sighed once again and moved his hat back and forth in his hands. 'But I haven't found any of them yet.'

'I'm so sorry, Uncle,' Emily said.

‘Thank you, Emily,’ Uncle Rolly replied. ‘When people say sorry it tells me they care and helps me to heal.’

There was a moment of silence, broken by the twitter of fairy wrens. Uncle Rolly turned to a bush and pointed at the darting brown shapes.

‘There you go.’ He clapped his hands. ‘They’re reminding us that there’s still lots to be happy for.’ He smiled. ‘Now, are you ready for today’s story?’

‘Yes please,’ both children said, and Ms Green nodded as well.

A WOMBAT'S TALE

'Ha ha, Birrin, you'll never catch us.'

Squeals rang across the clearing as Birrin the wombat chased his friends this way and that.

Although he was a very broad animal, Birrin could run very fast. He could run faster than the echidna, possum and goanna. He was even faster than the snake. In fact, he could run almost as fast as the emu, who was known by all the other animals as being very fast.

But although he could run fast, Birrin wasn't very nimble, and so he found it hard to tag any of his friends when they played. As he got close to them, they would move left or right at the last minute to avoid him.

Despite not being very good at tag, Birrin was always the first to put his paw up to play. He loved playing with his cousins, and they loved playing with him. They played early in the morning before the Elders sat them down and shared stories. They played in the afternoon after the Elders had finished teaching them about the Lore. Sometimes, when there was a full moon, they were allowed to play under the light of the stars.

One morning, while the children were sitting with the Elders, they noticed a new face in their circle.

'Everybody, this is Munyang,' Grandmother Kangaroo said to the group. 'He will be living with us for a little while.'

'Hello, Munyang,' the group said together in a cheerful tone to the water rat. Munyang didn't say anything. He just sat there with a smirk on his face.

Over the next few weeks, the children went out of their way to make Munyang feel welcome. He became so popular that he even formed his own group of friends. There was Baray the rock wallaby, Bilu the possum, Djurrgal the echidna and Mukin the bandicoot. The new group thought they were so cool they no longer played with the others.

One sunny afternoon, Munyang's gang sat on a small hill and watched the others play tag.

'Look at those silly kids,' Munyang said. 'And look at the stupid Birrin. His bum is so big it blocks out the sun.' They all pointed at Birrin and laughed.

Birrin noticed the group pointing at him and laughing. It made him feel very uncomfortable.

That night when the camp had all gone to bed, a group of small shadows crept into the bush.

No one saw them except for Birrin. He was very worried.

Should I go and wake the Elders? he thought. *Oh, what should I do?* He squeezed the sides of his head with his paws, but no answers came.

He decided to follow the group from a distance to make sure they were okay. As they moved further from camp, Birrin could hear Munyang's voice getting louder and louder.

'Stupid Old People,' Munyang cackled. 'Telling us things will grab us in the dark if we leave camp. I'm sick of their fairy tales.'

Birrin stopped on a small hill that ran down into a clearing, where the group stood around a fire.

Munyang was holding a large clump of grass over his bottom and waddling back and forth. 'Who am I?' he said.

'Fat bum Birrin,' one of his friends replied. They were laughing so hard they didn't notice a furry figure entering the clearing.

'Well, well. What have we here?' Batjigan said as he strolled towards the fire. Birrin could see more shapes emerging from the darkness behind the dingo. His heart started to beat very fast.

'They are in big trouble,' he whispered to himself. 'What should I do?' In an instant, he started digging, his strong shoulders and long claws slicing through the ground with ease. As Birrin dug, he watched the dingo walk towards the group.

'Looks like a bit of a party going on, hey?' Batjigan smiled a crooked smile. Rows of sharp teeth glistened.

'Yeah, well, don't go getting any ideas.' Munyang was trying to sound brave, but he looked terrified. 'The Elders know where we are, and they'll hear us if I yell out to them.'

'Is that so?' Batjigan's nose was almost touching Munyang's nose, the dingo's hot breath misty in the cool night air. The water rat's whiskers started to quiver.

'Hey, you Elders,' Batjigan yelled. 'What do you reckon about these boys way out here on their own?'

The other dingoes started to move into the firelight. 'Hey, Elders,' one of them jeered. 'You might want to come right now, or these kids might be in trouble. Because we're going to eat them.'

Batjigan hurled himself at the water rat's neck. Then there was a thump as Birrin's stout body collided with the dingo, throwing Batjigan into the air.

'Quick, follow me.' Birrin sprinted up the hill and stood next to the tunnel he had made. 'Climb down and I'll protect you.' Munyang, Baray, Bilu, Djurrgal and Mukin dived into the hole, Birrin close in behind them. The wombat could hear the group crying. 'Don't worry, you fullas. I've got this,' he said as he wedged himself into the hole and used his bottom to close the entrance.

Growls turned to howls as the dingoes bit and scratched at Birrin's exposed backside. No matter what they did, the wombat didn't move. The dingoes yelled nasty things at Birrin, but Birrin ignored them.

'They can carry on as much as they want,' he said to the animals huddled below him. His voice was very calm. 'Wombat bums are not only big, they're also as solid as tree trunks.'

The next morning, when the camp awoke and noticed the children were missing, scouts were sent out to find them. There was a whoop of joy when they came across a mound of dirt and next to it a hairy and scratched wombat's bottom.

That night, the camp held a huge corroboree to celebrate Birrin's courage, his quick thinking and above all, his big bum.

And he was never made fun of again.

HAVING a YARN

When Uncle Rolly finished the story, Jacob spoke first, golden syrup still dripping off his chin from the Johnny cakes.

'I feel happy for Birrin. The others were mean to him, but he turned out to be a hero.'

Uncle Rolly nodded. 'What made you think that?'

'Well,' Jacob replied. 'He was always positive. He didn't judge. He was kind.'

'He thought about others,' Emily added. 'He was humble and he was brave.'

'And what did you think about the water rat?' Uncle Rolly asked.

Emily spoke straight away. 'He was kind of the opposite to Birrin, wasn't he? He wasn't nice and he said nasty things.'

'And he wanted to be the centre of attention and he judged others,' Jacob added.

Smoke rose from the dying fire and surrounded them.

Uncle Rolly poked the coals with a stick and flames erupted. Jacob held out his freshly washed hands to dry while Emily watched a trail of smoke waft upwards and outwards, coating leaves and branches of nearby trees in a soft mist and making the sun change colour.

'To Aboriginal people,' Uncle Rolly said, 'the fire is alive, like us. It can be our friend if we give it boundaries, but if we let it do its own thing, a fire can become greedy and get out of control. That's why Aboriginal people have the Lore. The Lore gives us rules to live by so we can keep everything in balance.'

'What kind of rules?' Jacob asked. 'When I see my Uncle Joe, he tells me he is going to teach me the Lore, but he has never told me what it is.'

'The Lore teaches us many things, Jacob,' Uncle Rolly replied. 'But it is mainly about caring for our place and all things in our place; not being greedy; being humble, loving and respectful in all things that you do; and always sharing.'

'Munyang and his friends didn't follow the Lore, did they?'

The children were shocked that Ms Green had spoken.

'No, they didn't, Ms Green,' Uncle Rolly said, looking at her. 'Instead of being kind to Birrin, they were mean to him and called him names.'

'Just like the kids did at my school when I was young,' Ms Green added. Her face was very pale and her eyes sad.

'Yes. I know how that feels. I've had nasty things said to me over the years because of the colour of my skin.' Uncle Rolly held up his hand and looked at it intently. 'What happened at the milk bar wasn't the only time I've been treated differently to non-Aboriginal people. I've been in banks and shops where people wouldn't serve me.' He sat up straight and smiled. 'But I'm proud of my skin, and the rest of me as well. See, you're born the way you are for a reason. Look at Birrin. Those kids poked fun at his bottom, but it ended up saving them.'

The children smiled.

After saying goodbye to Uncle Rolly, the children

walked to Ms Green's car with the smell of smoke lingering in their nostrils, and the sounds of the bush caressing their ears, each lost in their own thoughts. Ms Green was deep in thought too. Uncle Rolly had given them all a lot to think about.

How would your life be different if you or your brothers or sisters were taken from your family?

Why is bullying not okay?

What can you do if you are being bullied or see someone else being bullied?

CONVERSATION POINT

ACTIVITY

Love Your Body

Social media, television and magazines can make you want to look different to how you are. It's hard to love the way you look sometimes, but it's important to look in the mirror and like what you see.

THINGS YOU WILL NEED:

- Coloured pencils, crayons or markers
- Paper or cardboard.

1. Draw a picture of yourself onto your paper or cardboard.
2. Write nice comments on your drawing about the different parts of your body. For example: 'Thank you feet for allowing me to stand up'; 'Thank you eyes for letting me see'; 'Thank you heart for pumping my blood'.

CHAPTER 5

EMILY AND JACOB were initially disappointed when Uncle Rolly had to cancel their next meeting. But their disappointment was forgotten when Ms Green told them they'd be going on another drive out into the bush to see Uncle Rolly next time.

It seemed to take forever for Ms Green's car to make its way along the windy road up into the mountains. When they finally arrived at their destination, their boredom turned to excitement as they saw Uncle Rolly's battered old car approaching in the distance.

'I think you fullas have grown taller since I've been away,' Uncle Rolly said once he had climbed from his car.

'Geez, Uncle. You haven't been away that long,' Jacob said.

'Where did you go?' Emily asked.

'Up north.' Uncle Rolly's voice was quiet. 'Sometimes things happen that we don't expect, ay.' He shook his head. 'Ah well. We're here now.' He tightened the straps on the small backpack he was wearing. 'I hope you're feeling fit, you fullas. We've got a bit of a walk ahead.'

They walked through dense undergrowth, taking great care

not to get caught up in the lantana. They stopped on top of a small rocky hill for a water break.

'The bush wasn't always like this, you know,' Uncle Rolly said. 'Our Old People used fire to keep the forest floor clean. This lantana was introduced to our country in 1841 to make someone's garden look nice.' He plucked a pink-and-yellow flower and stared at it. 'So pretty and yet so bad for the bush.'

They continued walking along a ridge into a forest filled with huge trees and canopies that filled the sky. Fingers of sunlight pierced the leafy covering with spears that sparkled and danced.

'Look around you,' Uncle Rolly said.

Surrounding them was a circle of trees with trunks as wide as cars. They were so tall, their tops couldn't be seen, and they had so many branches reaching out in all directions it was impossible to count them all.

'Close your eyes and tell me what you feel,' Uncle Rolly continued.

'I feel like I'm being watched.' Ms Green was the first to speak.

'I feel like I'm being cuddled,' Emily said.

'I didn't feel anything,' Jacob said. 'But in my mind, I saw an old woman with ochre on her face. I think it was my grandmother. My dad has a photo of her.'

'That doesn't surprise me, Jacob. See, we call these "grandmother trees"', Uncle Rolly told the children. 'These old women have been here for a long time.'

'Hello,' Emily whispered.

'I've been sitting with them since I was young. They've always been here for me, and they'll always be here for you.' He closed his eyes.

'Are you all right, Uncle?' Emily face was etched with concern. Jacob and Ms Green looked worried as well.

'I'm good now. I'm here with my family,' he replied, opening his eyes. 'Now, are you ready for a story?'

All was quiet except for the rustle of the trees. A wind was building.

Ochre is a
mineral in the
ground that can be
gathered as a rock
or in the form of clay,
and then crushed and
mixed with water
to create a kind
of paint.

A ROCKY TIME

From when Gutji was a child, he was always throwing rocks at things. No matter how many times he was told not to, he just couldn't stop.

'Gutji. You must stop throwing rocks,' his grandmothers would tell him.

'But I'm not throwing them at anybody,' he would reply. 'And look, I'm so good at it,' as he threw another rock into the bush.

'Gutji. There could be someone walking in the bush, and you might hit them,' he would be told. 'And there are other things in the bush that don't want you doing this. If you don't stop, you might get yourself into trouble.'

Gutji's best friend was Girrgirr the king parrot. Everyone thought it was funny that a lizard and a parrot could be best friends, but that didn't worry Gutji and Girrgirr. They did everything together.

Sometimes Girrgirr would soar into the sky and look for areas where the rocks were smooth and round, just how Gutji liked them.

One day, Girrgirr found a mound of rocks a short distance from a creek.

'Come, come, Gutji,' Girrgirr said, his wings fluttering with excitement. 'You won't believe what I've found for you.'

When Gutji made it to the rocks, he couldn't believe his eyes. 'There are so many rocks here,' he gasped. Gutji scuttled up the mound so quickly he scraped his knees. He stood at the

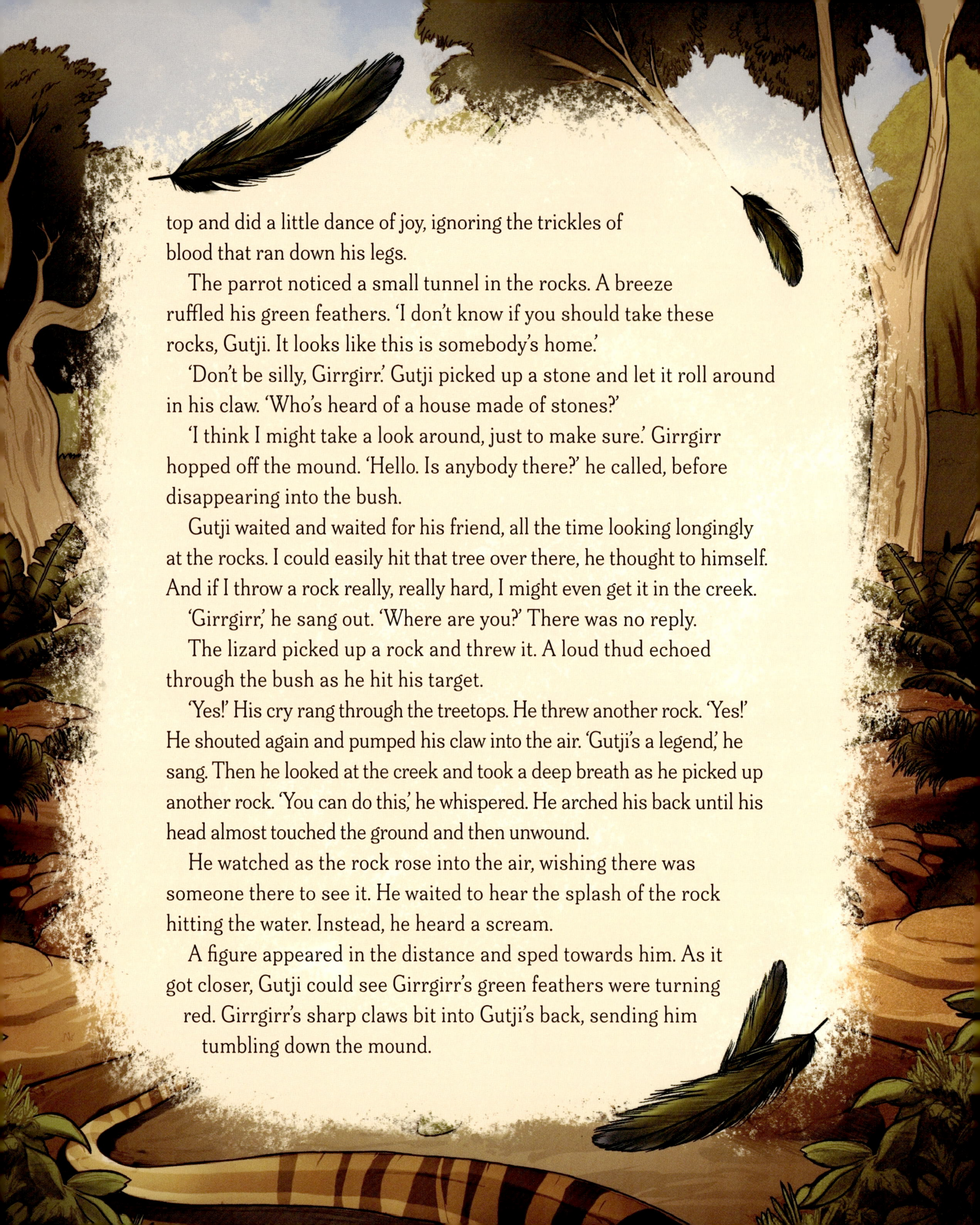

top and did a little dance of joy, ignoring the trickles of blood that ran down his legs.

The parrot noticed a small tunnel in the rocks. A breeze ruffled his green feathers. 'I don't know if you should take these rocks, Gutji. It looks like this is somebody's home.'

'Don't be silly, Girrgirr.' Gutji picked up a stone and let it roll around in his claw. 'Who's heard of a house made of stones?'

'I think I might take a look around, just to make sure.' Girrgirr hopped off the mound. 'Hello. Is anybody there?' he called, before disappearing into the bush.

Gutji waited and waited for his friend, all the time looking longingly at the rocks. I could easily hit that tree over there, he thought to himself. And if I throw a rock really, really hard, I might even get it in the creek.

'Girrgirr,' he sang out. 'Where are you?' There was no reply.

The lizard picked up a rock and threw it. A loud thud echoed through the bush as he hit his target.

'Yes!' His cry rang through the treetops. He threw another rock. 'Yes!' He shouted again and pumped his claw into the air. 'Gutji's a legend,' he sang. Then he looked at the creek and took a deep breath as he picked up another rock. 'You can do this,' he whispered. He arched his back until his head almost touched the ground and then unwound.

He watched as the rock rose into the air, wishing there was someone there to see it. He waited to hear the splash of the rock hitting the water. Instead, he heard a scream.

A figure appeared in the distance and sped towards him. As it got closer, Gutji could see Girrgirr's green feathers were turning red. Girrgirr's sharp claws bit into Gutji's back, sending him tumbling down the mound.

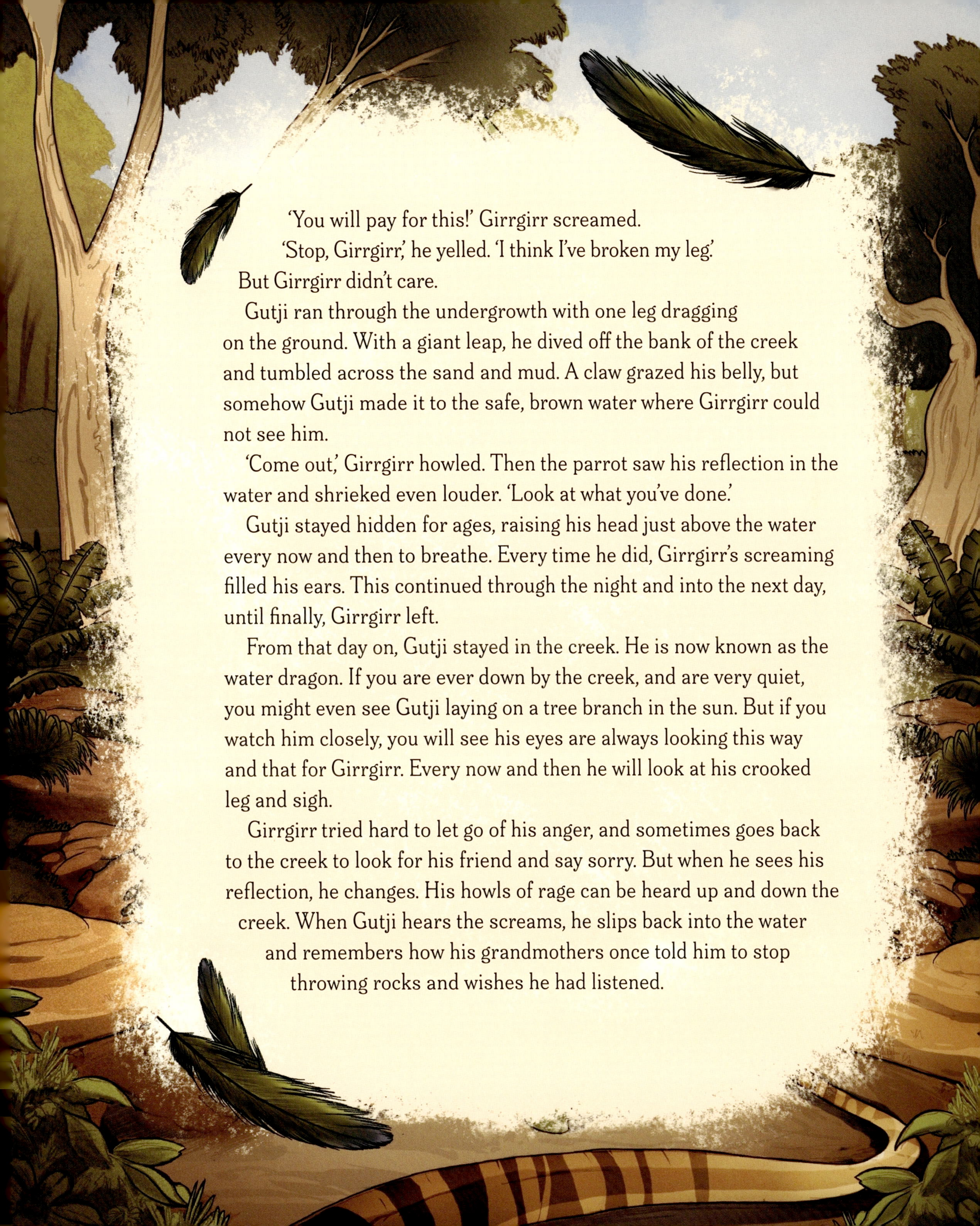

'You will pay for this!' Girrgirr screamed.

'Stop, Girrgirr,' he yelled. 'I think I've broken my leg.'

But Girrgirr didn't care.

Gutji ran through the undergrowth with one leg dragging on the ground. With a giant leap, he dived off the bank of the creek and tumbled across the sand and mud. A claw grazed his belly, but somehow Gutji made it to the safe, brown water where Girrgirr could not see him.

'Come out,' Girrgirr howled. Then the parrot saw his reflection in the water and shrieked even louder. 'Look at what you've done.'

Gutji stayed hidden for ages, raising his head just above the water every now and then to breathe. Every time he did, Girrgirr's screaming filled his ears. This continued through the night and into the next day, until finally, Girrgirr left.

From that day on, Gutji stayed in the creek. He is now known as the water dragon. If you are ever down by the creek, and are very quiet, you might even see Gutji laying on a tree branch in the sun. But if you watch him closely, you will see his eyes are always looking this way and that for Girrgirr. Every now and then he will look at his crooked leg and sigh.

Girrgirr tried hard to let go of his anger, and sometimes goes back to the creek to look for his friend and say sorry. But when he sees his reflection, he changes. His howls of rage can be heard up and down the creek. When Gutji hears the screams, he slips back into the water and remembers how his grandmothers once told him to stop throwing rocks and wishes he had listened.

HAVING A YARN

'Do you fullas know what the word "danger" means?' Uncle Rolly asked.

'Yeah, I get told all the time I can't do something because it's dangerous,' Jacob rolled his eyes. 'I get it. This story is about being safe, so we don't hurt ourselves or other people.'

'Life is very fragile,' Uncle Rolly said gently. 'It's so easy to get hurt. So, you need to always be looking out for that danger fulla, even when you're doing things you love and that you've done many times before.'

'What do you love doing, Uncle?' Emily asked.

'Well, I love walking and sitting in the bush.'

Emily laughed. 'That's not very dangerous is it, so you've got nothing to worry about.'

'Well, I don't want to fall over, or get lost, or get bitten by a snake. So, I still have to be careful, ay.'

'Mum doesn't like me going outside on my own,' Emily replied. 'You know, stranger danger.'

'Things have changed from when I was a kid. On the Reserve, we were always outside. Mainly because our houses only had one room.'

He laughed.

'What did you do outside?' Jacob asked.

'Lots of things,' Uncle Rolly replied. 'We played with toys we made out of powdered milk cans, and we played hopscotch and plug the duck. And sometimes, when it was hot and the Reserve Manager was in a good mood, he would let us go down to the river. We loved it there.'

He closed his eyes and smiled as he remembered. 'The long summer days of heat and dragonflies. The laughter up and down the waterway as we splashed and explored. Lying on the cool sand and watching the clouds say hello.'

'That sounds fun, but I bet you wish you had video games when you were a kid.' Jacob pretended he was using a console.

'I wouldn't even know how to use one, but sometimes we would see the non-Aboriginal kids playing with toy cars and we'd wish we were that lucky.' Uncle Rolly gently rubbed the large tree root he was sitting next to.

'But we had lots of fun, anyways, especially when we were allowed to go outside the fence. We'd climb trees, make swings, explore the bush. We never got bored, that's for sure.' He brushed a fly away from his face. 'But because we were told the Girrgirr and Gutji story when we were little, we were always careful not to do things that could hurt others.'

'I feel sorry for Girrgirr. He was trying to help his friend, and he ended up getting hurt,' Emily said.

'Yeah, but it was an accident,' Jacob added. 'And when Gutji said sorry, Girrgirr just wanted to hurt him back. That's not being a very good friend, is it?'

'Sometimes anger can lead to people hurting each other,' Uncle Rolly said. 'Sometimes anger can even lead to wars. Our Old People teach us to think about why we are angry and then deal with it so it doesn't hang around.'

He looked upwards through the deep green canopy. 'These old grandmother trees have helped me a lot with my anger over the years. They help me heal so that when I start thinking about my brothers and sisters who were taken all those years ago, I don't let hatred control me like it did with Girrgirr.'

As you get older and do more things on your own, what kinds of dangers do you need to be aware of?

CONVERSATION POINT

What can you do to make sure you don't put yourself, or your friends, in danger?

Do you think being angry can be dangerous?

What are good ways to deal with feeling angry?

ACTIVITY

Exercise

Walking Country is a great way to connect with nature and let go of worry and anger. It's also a great form of exercise. Exercise is good for both our bodies and our minds.

1. On the top of your poster, write the words, 'Exercise and Me'.
2. On the left-hand side of your poster, write down reasons why exercise is good for you.
3. Find pictures of exercises you can do outside. Print or cut them out and glue them onto the right-hand side of your poster (leave some space at the bottom). The pictures might be of someone playing sport, doing yoga, riding a bike, skipping rope, walking, running, swimming or something else.
4. Look at all the pictures and pick the things you would like to do the most.
5. Do your best to try each of the activities you have chosen (you might need the help of a parent or adult for some things).
6. Once you have done the different activities, on the bottom of your poster, write down the things you would like to do again.

THINGS YOU WILL NEED:

- Coloured pencils, crayons or markers
- Scissors
- Glue
- A blank poster-size piece of coloured cardboard.

CHAPTER 6

EMILY LIVED IN A NEAT, four-bedroom home overlooking a river. Jacob lived in a public housing unit nestled among twenty-five other units. Both children were excited to be visiting Uncle Rolly's house.

'I think his house will have a verandah,' Jacob said.

'I think it will have a nice garden,' Emily added.

They were both right. Uncle Rolly's house was small and old, sitting in a street of homes that were built by the government long ago. The front gate glistened with recently applied black paint and behind the fence was a garden full of flowers that splashed colour in all directions. The grass was trim and green. Along both side fences, numerous grevilleas were in flower, native birds twittering and chirping from their branches. The children and Ms Green were greeted at the door by Uncle Rolly, and were soon seated around the kitchen table.

'There you go, bub,' Uncle Rolly's wife, Lorraine, said as she placed the last glass of orange juice down on the table. 'I'll leave you fullas alone.'

Uncle Rolly watched his wife walk out of the room. His face was glowing. 'We been married nearly sixty years,' he said.

'Bub' is a word Aboriginal people sometimes use to show a person they care for them.

'Wow,' Jacob's eyes widened. 'I've never met people who've been together for that long!'

'You have a really cool house, Uncle,' Emily said. She looked around the room one more time. There were photographs everywhere. 'Are they all family?'

'For Aboriginal people, everyone is mob one way or another,' Uncle Rolly said with a grin.

He pulled out a photograph from the top pocket of his shirt. It was brown and crinkled.

Aboriginal people sometimes use the word 'mob' as another way of saying they are connected to each other as a group or family.

'I always keep this in my pocket so it's close to my heart.' He laid it on the table so everyone could see it.

'This was my family when

I was a little boy. It's the only photograph I have. That's me there.' A thin, shaky finger pointed to a small figure who looked no more than six years old. 'Look at those skinny legs poking out of those big baggy shorts.'

He laughed. 'I don't know how those legs carried me around. But that's the trick, see. Sometimes we need other people when we are carrying a burden. Which kind of relates to today's story. Are you ready?'

A FAMILY TREE

Gulawayn had been in his mother's pouch for six months before climbing onto her back, where he spent many more months asking all sorts of questions so he could be ready to do things on his own.

When this finally happened, Gulawayn got busy exploring. He explored his tree, and then he explored the tree next to his. After that, he explored another tree, and then another.

After a while, he became brave enough to explore other parts of the bush. He was always excited when he came across another koala, but he also enjoyed meeting other animals.

'When you see those other animals, always remember they're family,' his mother had told him. 'They're all your cousins.'

Gulawayn met feathered cousins, furred cousins, cousins that were cold blooded, and cousins that were hot blooded. He met cousins who lived in the water, cousins who lived in the earth, and cousins who spent a lot of time in the sky. They were all very different, but within the differences he found there was a sameness. His favourite cousins were the girrga, the native bees. Although koala bears weren't supposed to eat honey, Gulawayn was the exception. He loved it more than anything.

By the time Gulawayn became an adult, he had made many special friendships.

His most special friendship was with Marrung. She was fun to be with and very caring. While sitting around the fire one night, he looked at her and realised that he was in love with her.

After everyone had left, he told his grandmother of his feelings.

'I'm so sorry, bub,' she said. 'You can't marry Marrung. She's not the right blood.'

Gulawayn's head dropped. 'Yes. I understand, my gimbi.'

With an aching heart, Gulawayn's grandmother watched her grandson disappear into the darkness.

When Gulawayn was far away from the camp, he allowed his tears to flow. He cried through the night. He cried through the day. He cried until there were no more tears, and then he cried some more.

His friend Wannga the riflebird saw him crying and asked what was wrong.

'I'm sorry that you are so unhappy,' Wannga said. 'How about I dance for you to cheer you up?'

Wannga danced and danced, but it did nothing to lift Gulawayn's mood.

Gukandi the kookaburra came down to help. 'I shall tell you some jokes, Gulawayn. That will cheer you up.' But Gulawayn was still miserable.

Pretty soon there were many animals doing all sorts of things to try and lift the little koala's spirits. But nothing worked.

Gulaiwayn appreciated what everyone was doing, but all he could think about was how sad he felt.

Eventually the feeling of emptiness moved to his belly. *I need some honey,* he thought. *That always makes me feel better.*

He made his way to a tree where some girrga lived and told them how sad he felt and why.

'We are your friends, Gulawayn,' a girrga Elder told him. 'We are happy to share our honey with you.'

Gulawayn ate the honey and felt much better. 'Thank you, my friends,' he said, before finding a nice gum tree he could nestle in and go to sleep. As he was sleeping, he started to dream about Marrung. He awoke and started to cry. I need more honey, he thought.

He visited the girrga again and asked for more honey.

'No, Gulawayn,' the girrga Elder said. 'You know the Lore. All food is sacred. Eating too much honey because you are sad isn't good for you. Now go back to your home where there are people who can help you with your sadness.'

But Gulawayn wasn't interested in getting help from his Elders. All he could think about was honey. So, he waited for the bees to leave their nest for an evening corroboree, then he climbed their tree and ate all their honey before disappearing into the night.

When the girrga returned to find their hive empty of honey, they spoke to dhurrgung the owl, who watches over everything. Night after night, Gulawayn would find a hive of the girrga and eat all their honey, travelling further and further away from his home. It took his family many weeks to find him.

'Come down and talk to us, Gulawayn,' his sister pleaded. But he ignored her.

'Go away, all of you,' he yelled. 'I don't need anybody. Leave me alone.'

'Gulawayn. Please come down and talk to me,' a soft voice said. He looked down. Marrung's shoulders were slumped and her eyes very sad. 'I'm so worried about you.'

'We can never be together, Marrung.' Gulawayn's tears flowed as he climbed down the tree and walked past her. 'I'm sorry. I will head west over the mountains, so I no longer hurt you or my people.'

And that is what Gulawayn did.

But Gulawayn's family never gave up on him, and with the help of Dhurrgung the owl, they were able to ask the animals on his western path to be there for him. Even the girrga gave him support and encouragement.

Over time, his need for lots of honey disappeared. He also made many new friends, including a koala named Bangayal, who enjoyed his stories and thought he was funny. They eventually fell in love and had many children, who loved to explore and meet new people just like their father.

And on special occasions, Gulawayn and his children visit the girrga for a yarn, and just a little bit of honey.

HAVING A YARN

Uncle Rolly looked down at the old photograph of him and his family. 'This is a sad story.' He kissed the picture and put it gently back in his pocket. 'But sometimes sad things happen.' He looked out the window at a honeyeater feeding from a bright orange grevillea flower. 'So, what did you learn from Gulawayn's story?'

Ms Green spoke before Jacob or Emily could answer. 'That sad times are a part of our life, but they don't need to be our entire life,' she said.

'As Ms Green said, we all get sad sometimes,' Uncle Rolly said. 'But we don't want it to stay for too long.' He looked at

Ms Green and smiled. 'Sometimes we can be sad and not even know it. That's why our friends are so important. They can help us see what we don't see.'

Ms Green looked startled for a moment, then she smiled back and seemed suddenly more relaxed.

Uncle Rolly continued speaking. 'So, when we are unhappy or stressed, it can be easy to give up or feel sorry for ourselves. We call that giving away our power. Another way to think of it is giving away our happiness. People give away their power to fear, alcohol, gambling, mobile phones, all sorts of things. You can even give away your power to video games.' He winked at Jacob, whose face went red. 'The question to ask is, am I in control of this thing or is it in control of me?'

'So,' Emily said. 'Gulawayn was in control of how much honey he ate, and then it was in control of him, and then, with the help of his family and friends, he was in control again.'

'That's right,' Uncle Rolly replied. 'I've been where this story sits in Country, ay. It's a special place and there's a big stone that looks like a koala.'

'No way,' Jacob said.

He came back to the table with a framed photograph and pointed at it. 'What can you see?'

'I can see you and Aunty Lorraine and lots of kids,' Jacob replied.

'What can you see in the background?'

Both children squinted and stared. Then Emily's eyes nearly popped out of her head.

'It's a mountain, but it looks like a lizard,' she said.

'That's right. We share stories when we're sitting around the fire, but the land has many stories in it as well.'

'So, this mountain has a story about a lizard?' Jacob was shaking his head.

'It sure does,' Uncle Rolly replied. 'His name is Makang. You never know. I might take you there one day.'

'Actually,' Ms Green looked excited, 'I've got good news.' Her eyes sparkled. 'We have special permission for an overnight trip to this site.'

Emily clapped. Jacob did as well.

Ms Green looked at Uncle Rolly with a huge grin. 'I'm sorry, Uncle. I wanted to tell you first, but I just couldn't hold it in.'

'That's all right, bub.' Uncle Rolly smiled. 'I could do with a bit of excitement at the moment.'

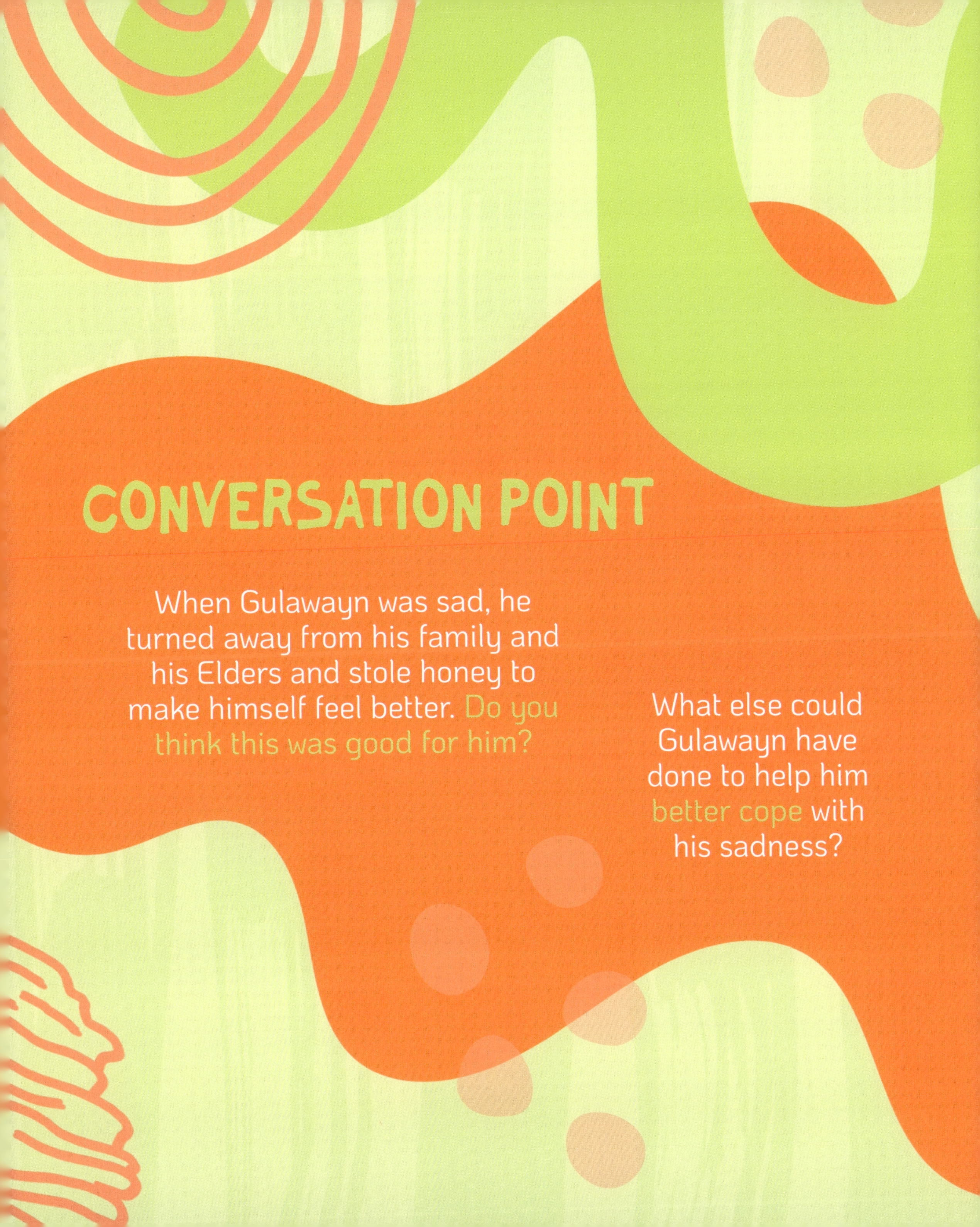

CONVERSATION POINT

When Gulawayn was sad, he turned away from his family and his Elders and stole honey to make himself feel better. Do you think this was good for him?

What else could Gulawayn have done to help him better cope with his sadness?

ACTIVITY

The Power of Story

THINGS YOU WILL NEED:

- Access to the internet with an adult to help
- Access to a library or bookshop
- Access to Aboriginal Elders or Aboriginal story holders
- A pen
- A blank piece of paper.

Aboriginal stories can entertain us as well as teach us more about the way we think and act.

1. Using any of the items listed, access five traditional Aboriginal stories. If possible, try to find stories from your local area. It's okay if you can't.
2. Read each story and write down what you think it's trying to teach you.
3. Discuss with a parent or teacher.
4. Decide whether the story has a message you can use in your day-to-day life.

CHAPTER 7

JACOB, EMILY, MS GREEN and even Uncle Rolly were counting down the days to their trip to Makang Mountain. It was Emily and Jacob's first time camping and they were beyond excited.

When the day finally arrived, they spent the afternoon setting up the tents, cooking beef stew in a camp oven, and making billy tea and damper. When night fell, they sat around the fire together.

'I never knew there were so many stars,' Emily said, her head tilted back so far it looked like she might fall out of her chair.

'And I didn't know the stars make patterns.' Jacob pointed. 'There's a pot.'

'In the day, Country shows us lots of story,' Uncle Rolly said. 'And at night, the stars do the same. No matter where we are or what time it is, we are surrounded by story.'

With the comforting smell of smoke in their hair, each of the group faded off to sleep with a happy heart and a peaceful mind.

The following morning, after a big breakfast of bacon and eggs cooked in a cast-iron pan that looked as old as Uncle Rolly, the group followed a bush track that went past rocky cliffs, over chattering streams and into a large forest of gum trees.

'Not far now.' Uncle Rolly walked along the track with ease, while Jacob, Emily and Ms Green struggled to catch their breath.

They eventually walked out of the cover of the eucalyptus trees onto a clearing of fine red dust on the edge of a cliff. Above them was a perfect blue sky; below them, a valley of rainforest.

'Close your eyes,' Uncle Rolly said. 'Keep them closed, and turn around and face the way you came in.' The three moved like a trained marching band. 'Now, open your eyes and look up.'

'Wow,' Jacob said.

Emily stared without saying a word.

The mountain loomed over them, a silent, giant sentinel watching over the land, solid and infinite. The reptile's head was looking at them, each stony eye as large as a truck, very much alive and full of menace. Its body bridged numerous valleys and its tail swept down to distant blue-green hills coated in haze.

'Well, everybody,' Uncle Rolly whispered. 'With much respect, I would like to introduce you to Makang.'

A murder of crows sat watching the group from the twisted branches of a dead tree.

Uncle Rolly looked up at them and nodded. 'I see you, Waagan.' He looked back at the children. 'They're here to welcome you.'

'It feels really old here.' Jacob rubbed his arm, deep in thought.

'I feel a little bit scared, but I also feel a little bit happy,' Emily said.

Uncle Rolly looked over to Ms Green.

Ms Green looked back. 'I feel very blessed to be here,' she said, and the two smiled at each other.

The four allowed the silence to cover them.

After a while, Uncle Rolly spoke. 'Well, you fullas. I've told you many stories about many things, and now you're ready to hear the biggest story of all. You are ready to find out how it all began.'

THE BEGINNING

Once upon a time, way back in the beginning, the planet Earth was totally covered by water. But under the water was the land, our Mother, fast asleep.

Inside the Mother's belly, the rainbow serpent, Waawai, started to move and the Mother woke. From deep down under the water, she began to move upwards.

Eventually the land rose up out of the sea. The waters broke and the Mother was born.

When Biaimii, our sky Father, saw the Mother appear out of the ocean, he was amazed.

'In all the time I have been looking out over the universe, I have never seen anything so beautiful,' he said. 'I must go down to this place and see what it is.'

He came down from the sky and met the Mother. They shared time together and got to know each other. At first, they became friends, and then they fell in love.

But Biaimii had responsibilities that meant he had to go back to the sky. Although he wanted to spend more time with the Mother, with great sadness he had to leave her and return to his home.

From their great love, the Mother became pregnant and eventually the first children were born. They were great ancestral animals that walked country making mountains, valleys and all the landscapes we can see today.

It took a long time for this to happen, and there are many stories of how plants came to be, how animals came to be, how fish came to be, how birds came to be, how insects came to be, how all things came to be. Humans were the last of the children.

Every creature and every thing comes from the Mother and has story. The sky, the sun, the moon and the stars have story also. The stories explain that each of us is connected to all things. We are one.

HAVING A YARN

Uncle Rolly pointed at the mountain. 'That old lizard you can see; he's part of the Creation story I just told you. Now, you don't have to believe the story, but I would like you to respect that I believe it.'

Emily's eyes were shining. 'I could see the land rise out of the water, Uncle,' she said. 'And it looked beautiful.'

Uncle Rolly closed his eyes, took a deep breath and smiled. He opened his eyes and slowly moved in a circle, looking at everything around him.

'The land, our Mother, is sacred,' he said. 'The Mother is the most beautiful thing in the universe.' Uncle Rolly's voice trembled and there was a tear in his eye. 'If I sing for my Mother, if I dance for my Mother, if I learn all I can about my Mother, if I love my Mother, if I care for my Mother, then she will give me all that I need.'

He took off his hat, and his mop of white hair stirred in the breeze. With the slightest movement, he lifted one leg then stomped his foot gently into the dust. Then he did the same with the other leg.

The hairs on Jacob's arms stood up.

As he danced, Uncle Rolly sang. It started as a whisper but grew louder. His stomping became harder. Dust started to rise all around him. The dust hovered in the air long after he had finished the song.

'See that dust there,' he said. 'We dance to raise the dust so we can connect the Mother with the Father once more, to remind us that everything in Country comes from love, including us. Now, it's your turn to dance with me.'

Uncle Rolly sang the song once again. Emily and Jacob were moving in time with it almost instantly. Ms Green looked uncomfortable to start with, but after a while, she relaxed and seemed to move almost without thinking. Everyone was smiling when they had finished.

'That happiness you are feeling – that's the feeling you get when you connect with country,' Uncle Rolly said. He crouched and rubbed his hands into the dust. 'We come from the land so we must care for the land.' He stood and rubbed some of the dust onto his forehead. It left a mark that glowed in the sunlight.

'When we walk this land, it's important to tread softly and with respect, to not disturb anything, and leave nothing behind but our footprints.'

A large clattering noise filled the sky. They looked to where the noise came from and saw a machine digging into the mountain.

'We tried to stop that mine from happening,' Uncle Rolly said sadly. 'But no-one would listen. I use things that have been dug from the earth, but when I see how we have hurt the land, the rivers, the skies and the seas, my old heart aches.'

From overhead, there was a loud flutter of wings. The crows circled the group three times before diving into the valley below.

'In the Creation story, what was it that Biaimii had to do that made him sad?' Uncle Rolly asked.

Both children struggled to think of an answer and then Emily became very animated.

'He had to return to the sky when he really wanted to stay with the Mother.'

'That's right, Emily. Carrying out our responsibilities means we have to make hard decisions sometimes. But our responsibilities give us purpose so we don't become lost.'

'Lost?' Emily looked confused.

'When I am out and about, I see a lot of people who are so busy they forget what's important. They fall off the Dreaming Path and become unhappy.' Uncle Rolly looked at Emily and Jacob with eyes that blazed. 'I am hoping you fullas can help me remind people of their responsibility to care for their place, and all things in their place.'

'How?' Jacob replied. 'We're just two kids.'

Uncle Rolly pulled something out of his pocket. 'See this seed? If I plant it in the right soil and care for it, this seed will grow into the most beautiful tree.'

Uncle Rolly put the seed into Emily's hand. She closed her eyes and took a deep breath. She was still smiling when she carefully dropped the seed onto Jacob's outstretched hand. 'If the four of us start doing little things to care for the land and all things on the land, what do you think might happen?' Uncle Rolly asked.

'Well ...' Jacob scratched his head. 'Maybe others will notice?'

Uncle Rolly nodded. 'And they might tell others. So, the number of people caring and sharing grows.'

Jacob handed back the precious seed with great care. 'Uncle,' he said, 'is there a reason why humans were the last children?'

Uncle Rolly returned the seed to his pocket. 'The reason why humans came last was to remind us that the Mother and her children are older than us and wiser than us.' Uncle Rolly swept his arm in a big circle, pointing to the forest that surrounded them. 'All these trees, animals and birds are our older brothers and sisters. They are our teachers.'

'We need to listen to them, don't we?' Emily said.

'I think there's a practical side to this as well,' Ms Green said. 'If we don't look after nature, we'll have nothing to eat, nothing to drink, nothing to breathe and nowhere to live.'

Uncle Rolly's face glowed. 'Yes, you're both right. We do need to listen to the Mother and her children. And I think the young people of the world are going to do just that.'

The four stood in silence once more, taking in the beauty that surrounded them one last time. Then Uncle Rolly clapped his hands together, making them all jump.

'Now. Ms Green, if you can start making your way back to the car, I've just got to spend a few minutes on my own if that's okay?'

Ms Green and the children were well out of sight when the Elder said his prayer.

'To my ancestors, to this place, I pay my respects and humble myself before you. Please give me the strength to accept whatever happens next.' He bowed his head and breathed in the sweet perfume of eucalyptus before walking back to the car with a spring in his step.

CONVERSATION POINT

Why do Aboriginal people refer to the planet as their 'Mother'?

How important are the land, sky and waters to life on earth?

How important are the land, sky and waters to you?

ACTIVITY

Your Special Place

In Aboriginal culture, the land is our Mother and everything on the land is family. The Old People tell us that sitting in nature is very good for us. It helps us to let go of stress, connect with what is around us and be happy.

1. Think about somewhere in nature you have visited that you love or somewhere you would like to go. It might be on the beach, next to a stream, in the mountains or somewhere else.
2. When you're ready, close your eyes and see this place in your mind. Notice what you can see, hear, smell and feel. Take as long as you like.

THINGS YOU WILL NEED:

- You.

This is your special place. You can visit it in your mind whenever you are stressed or sad and it can help you feel better.

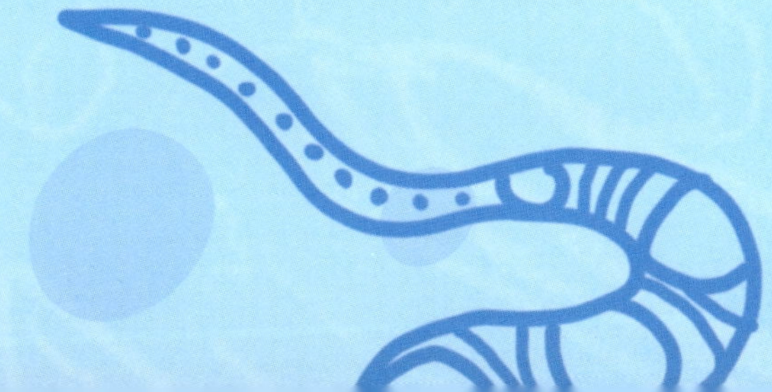

CHAPTER 8

EMILY AND JACOB were bored. They had met Uncle Rolly out in the bush, in his house and gone on an amazing trip to Makang Mountain. Sitting in an empty classroom felt like a bit of a let-down. Uncle Rolly was running late to meet them, which was unusual, and their boredom began to shift to worry.

Ms Green rang Uncle Rolly but there was no answer. The three looked out the classroom window waiting for him to appear, but there was no sign of him. Just as they were about to give up on the meeting, a familiar blue shirt appeared across the school grounds.

'Yes.' Jacob pumped his fist. The colour came back into Ms Green's cheeks and Emily clapped.

'Who's that with him?' Emily asked.

'I don't know.' Ms Green looked curiously out the window.

As he got closer, the trio could see the old man was even happier than usual. His hands were animated as he spoke to the figure by his side, and laughter shattered the silence that had blanketed the school grounds.

The stranger was easier to see now. She looked to be the same age as Uncle Rolly, but was shorter and wore a bright orange dress that glowed against her brown skin. She wore a brightly coloured headband in her flowing grey hair and her eyes shimmered in a soft and loving way.

Her face was kind but there were wrinkles and lines that promised stories of hardship.

'Hey there, my friends,' Uncle Rolly greeted them. 'Sorry I'm late. This is Carol, and she's my special guest today. We haven't seen each other for a little while, so I was telling her all about you fullas. And she pestered and pestered me to come and meet you.'

'Go away, Rolly. Shaming me up now.' The woman smiled in a nervous but happy way. 'It's lovely to meet you all.'

'Now, I reckon you want to know a bit more about Carol, so let me start by saying Carol likes to share yarns too,' Uncle Rolly said. 'So, I thought you might like to hear one of her stories. What do you think?'

'Yes, please.' The children's grins were almost as big as Uncle Rolly's.

BUTAN FINDS FAMILY

Butan the black snake had tried so very hard to hold it in, but he couldn't anymore. He lay by the waterhole and cried.

In his short life, he had faced much hardship. He had never known his mother or his father. He had never known his brothers or his sisters. He had never known anyone in his family. For as long as he could remember, he had been alone. Whenever he tried to say hello to other animals, they would run away screaming, 'Snake!' All he wanted in his life was a friend.

Sometimes he would watch the flocks of birds in the sky and wish he were up there without a care in the world. Sometimes he would sneak to the edge of a grassy pasture and watch a mob of kangaroos, sunning themselves and imagine lying with them. Sometimes he would sit on a cliff top and watch schools of fish glinting in the water below and wonder what it was like to have such a big family.

He knew watching the birds, kangaroos and fish made him feel even lonelier, but he did it anyway.

The sound of his crying floated up the steep banks of the waterhole to Grandmother Baaray.

'Who is so very, very sad?' the old blue tongue lizard said. 'It isn't right for someone to be so sad.' Grandmother Baaray was very old, so could only move slowly. As she got closer to the crying, she could see Butan's little body shaking. 'There, there,' the old lizard said gently. Butan was so startled that he almost slithered away. 'There's no need to be frightened, little one,' Grandmother Baaray said. 'I'm here to see why you're so sad.'

On hearing the old lizard's words, the little snake cried even harder. He had never known anyone to be kind to him.

Grandmother Baaray cradled Butan's head and rocked him. 'There, there, bub. I'm here now. You tell me what's wrong and we'll sort it out.'

After taking a deep breath, Butan told his story. As he spoke, he saw the care in the old lizard's eyes and his worries left. When he was finished, Grandmother Baaray continued to rock him.

'Well, you never have to be lonely again, bub,' she said. 'You can come back with me and be one of my grandchildren. But I need to warn you, I have many grandchildren, and they'll all want to be your friend. So be ready for lots of fuss.'

The little snake was nervous and excited when they reached the camp. He felt so shy that he didn't know what to do when he was introduced to everyone. He was also surprised when no-one yelled out in fear and ran away. Grandmother was right, they all made a big fuss over him.

Over the next few days, he and his new cousins played hide and seek in the long grass and they explored the rocky hill where cranky old frill necked lizard told them to go away. They

spent time down by the waterhole looking for platypus, and visited the lyrebird, who danced for them.

Butan had so much fun, but his favourite thing was sitting around the fire at night and listening to the Elders tell stories. He heard stories about the Lore, and learned to share and not be greedy. He heard stories about faraway places that he was told he would visit one day. He also heard about the connection between the Black Snake people and the Blue Tongue Lizard people and got very excited.

One night, just before he fell asleep, he realised how happy he was. His heart felt as if it were going to burst with the love he felt inside. He was finally able to let go of the bad memories of the past.

The next morning, he and Grandmother Baaray were sitting together waiting to watch the sun rise.

'Grandmother, can I tell you something?' he asked.

'Of course, you can, bub,' Grandmother replied.

'Meeting you has been the best thing ever. I love you.'

'I love you too. Meeting you has been very special for me as well.' After a while, the old blue tongue lizard spoke again. 'The Lore teaches us that we are created in love, we are born into love and, as we grow, we are surrounded by love.' She leaned over and kissed Butan on the top of his head. 'No matter how lonely you may feel, you are always loved.'

They both smiled. Words were not needed as the first fingers of light from grandmother sun bathed them in love.

HAVING A YARN

After she'd finished speaking, Carol looked to Uncle Rolly and nodded.

'You might be wondering who this wonderful storyteller is.'

Uncle Rolly smiled but his lips trembled and his eyes were watery. 'I'll give you a clue. She's good looking, like someone else you know.'

Emily and Jacob glanced at each other. They had no idea who she might be.

Tears were now running down Uncle Rolly's wrinkled cheeks, and the woman was crying as well. 'This is my sister, Carol.'

The children's jaws dropped.

'But, Uncle, I thought you didn't know any of your sisters or brothers,' Jacob said.

Carol's smile filled the room. 'He rang me five days ago and left a message telling me he thought I might be his sister.' She put a hand on her brother's arm. 'There wasn't a day when I didn't think about my family. I'd given up hope, but he hadn't.'

Uncle Rolly pulled out a crumpled and tattered handkerchief and blew his nose loudly.

'I was only two when I was taken,' Carol continued, 'and I was moved so far away. I couldn't remember where I came from. Meeting my big brother is the best thing to happen to me in my life.'

Brother and sister were now holding hands.

'And now I've found you, I'll never let you go.' Uncle Rolly's voice shook. Tears were flowing freely throughout the group now, and Ms Green passed around a box of tissues.

'We didn't get the chance to grow up together, but we're together now, and that's all that matters.' Uncle Rolly said. 'It turns out we have a lot in common, ay?'

'True,' Carol said. 'We both love corned meat with onion sauce, we both love being out in the bush and we both love watching movies.'

'And we both like telling Dreamtime stories,' Uncle Rolly added.

'The story about Butan is my favourite story yet,' Emily said.

Uncle Rolly looked at his sister and winked. 'Look out. You come in here for five minutes and they already like you more than me.'

'We like you both.' Jacob giggled.

'Before I met you, Uncle Rolly, I used to feel like Butan did.' Emily said. 'But I don't feel like that anymore. So, you are a bit like the grandmother lizard.'

'Loneliness is a big problem for many people, I'm afraid.' Carol looked at Emily and smiled.

'See, our culture is all about connection,' Uncle Rolly said. 'We care for each other, we care for Country, we care for everything on Country.'

'The more we connect with what's around us, the better our life is,' Carol added. The Creation Story that Rolly told you shows us that all living things are connected as family. So, no matter how unloved and lonely you may feel sometimes, in our way, you are always loved by your brothers, sisters and other family members in the bush, in the waterways and in the sky.'

Uncle Rolly turned to Ms Green. 'Now, Ms Green, you are very educated, so can I ask you a question?'

'Of course, Uncle.'

'Do you think the world would be a better place if everybody accepted their responsibility to care for their place and all things in their place, supported each other to live the best story possible and encouraged each other to build good relationships?'

'Yes, of course it would.' Ms Green nodded.

'That was Aboriginal society for thousands and thousands of years,' he continued.

'If you look at traditional Aboriginal society, there were no castles or forts,' Carol said. 'There were no armies, no one was poor, or homeless or went hungry.' Pride filled Uncle Rolly's eyes as he watched his sister speak. 'People who say Australia was discovered by Captain Cook make me laugh,' Carol continued without a smile. 'We were here long before that fulla, thank you very much. And we had all we needed to live a good life.'

'Now, you fullas, time is almost up for today, Uncle Rolly said, 'and I know next week will be our last meeting.' Both children's shoulders slumped. 'So, I need you to promise me you'll think about the good times we've had together, and share those thoughts when you do your presentation.'

Emily and Jacob nodded. Emily looked at Carol. 'Will we be seeing you next week, Aunty?'

'I'm sorry bub, I can't make it next week,' Carol replied. 'But I'm so pleased to have met you. You have made my brother so happy.'

Brother and sister said their goodbyes and left together, leaving Emily and Jacob to work on their presentation.

CONVERSATION POINT

Why was Butan sad?

What is a relationship?

Why are relationships important?

How do you care for and nourish a relationship?

ACTIVITY

Family

If birds, fish, insects, trees, lizards, kangaroos, people and everything else all come from one Mother, it means that they're all brothers and sisters. It means they're all family. It means we're never alone.

THINGS YOU WILL NEED:

- You
- An adult (parent or carer)
- Transport
- A place in nature to visit.

1. Ask a parent or carer if they can take you somewhere in nature where you can be away from the noise and rush of everyday life.
2. Find a space that feels nice to you or makes you feel happy.
3. Take your shoes off. While standing up, wriggle your feet and notice how it tickles but also feels good. Close your eyes and feel how connected you are to Mother Earth and smile.
4. Now, open your eyes and look at any plants or trees or flowers that are around you. Think about how they are family and smile.
5. Look and listen for animals or birds that may be around you. Think about how they are family and smile.
6. Say to yourself: 'I am loved and I am never alone'.

CHAPTER 9

MS GREEN LOOKED around the room. The same books were on the same shelves, and nothing had changed, unlike Ms Green, who felt like a new person. When she agreed to help the children with their project, she had no idea listening to Uncle Rolly would change her life. Three months before, she had been feeling lost and ready to give up teaching. But after many trips into the bush and connecting with Country, she had found her love for life again. She was happy for the children and happy for herself. Which made saying goodbye so sad.

Emily couldn't stop wriggling in her seat, but this time she didn't run her fingers through her hair. Instead, she placed her arms flat on the table and thought about the card she had made. She felt like Uncle Rolly had become part of her family.

Jacob flopped onto the table and buried his head into his crossed arms, deep in thought about how much he liked listening to Uncle Rolly. He was going to miss the yarns.

Uncle Rolly walked into the room. 'Goodness me, you two,' he said. 'You look like you dropped your ice creams on the ground!'

Ms Green had to dab her eyes with a tissue. Then she handed Uncle Rolly a cup of tea.

He sat down and slurped from it. 'So, today is a special day, and it's our final yarn. I've thought about many stories I could tell you and decided on a really important one that I think will finish off your project nicely. Are you ready?'

Everyone smiled.

A TALE OF TWO BROTHERS

Maalganbuki, who was always called Buki, and Maalganbudjari, who was always called Budjari, were brothers. In fact, they were identical twins and no-one, not even their mother, could tell them apart by looking at them. But from the moment they were born, they acted very differently.

Buki was very negative and never helped anyone. Budjari was positive about everything and always helping others.

'Budjari,' Buki used to say while rolling his eight eyes, 'you drive me crazy with your attitude.'

'What's wrong with my attitude, Buki?' Budjari would laugh and run over to give his brother a big hug. 'Maybe my attitude can rub off onto you.'

'Go away. The last thing I want is to be like you.' Buki would then scamper away into a dark corner to hide.

As the brothers grew up, they spent a lot of time with the Elders, who told them many stories and showed them many things. Budjari always looked and listened. Buki always fell asleep.

Many years passed, and the brothers were now grown-up.

'Can you believe this is the last night we will be living here?' Budjari said. His many legs danced. 'I can't wait to build my own place.'

'Go to sleep,' Buki replied.

The next day, Budjari set out with great excitement to find just the right location for his new home. His brother followed him, moaning about how it was too early to be doing such things.

'This looks like a great spot to build a web,' Budjari said. 'What do you think, Buki?'

'I don't like it,' the brother replied. 'It's out in the open and will get torn apart by the wind.'

'I'll give it a go, anyway.' Budjari worked hard all afternoon. His brother watched and shook his head. 'What do you think?' Budjari said when he'd finished his web. He looked very pleased.

'You've wasted your time,' Buki replied. 'You would have been far better off doing what I'm doing.'

'And what's that?' Budjari asked.

'Sitting under these rocks where I can be left alone,' Buki said in a cranky voice.

The next morning Budjari awoke with a start. He was swinging around in the wind like a trapeze artist.

'Ha, ha. I told you,' Buki said with a dry spider cackle.

'You're right,' Budjari replied. 'I need to build out of the wind.'

So Budjari found a more sheltered spot and spent all afternoon spinning a perfectly shaped web. As he worked, he sang a cheerful song his grandfather had taught him.

'Nope. You've picked the wrong spot,' Buki said. 'Waparr the kangaroo passes this way all the time. It will get torn down overnight.'

'Ah, well. It's done now,' Budjari replied.

As he looked at his brother, Buki had to rub all eight of his eyes. Budjari's body had become smaller and was now covered in the faintest of rainbows.

'Whatever,' Buki said as he crawled back into the rocks.

That night, Budjari awoke with a start. Something had run into his web, and once again he was swinging around in the air. He lowered himself to the ground and slept under a leaf for the rest of the night.

Buki found his brother the next morning, the broken web swaying to and fro above him.

'Ha, ha. I told you it would get torn down,' Buki crowed in an eerie spider way.

'You're right again, brother,' Budjari replied. 'I need to build out of the wind and away from where animals pass.'

And so this continued over a long time. Budjari would build a web that would fall apart or be torn apart, and Buki would laugh at him and tell him to live in the rocks.

Although Budjari failed many times, he learned from his mistakes. Each web was better than the last one. Each time he built a new web, he would do a little dance of joy. When he danced, his body would get smaller and the colours on his body would grow brighter.

Eventually he built the perfect web in the perfect place.

Although Budjari had learned many things, he had continued to sit with his Elders and learn from them, which his brother thought was a waste of time. Eventually Budjari became so full of knowledge and magical power, he didn't even need a web anymore.

In the past, when Budjari had failed, his brother had laughed at him. When Budjari had succeeded, his brother had become jealous. Now Budjari was powerful, Buki became angry. As his anger grew, his body became larger, and a red mark started to appear on his back.

The Elders told him, 'Don't hold onto that anger, Maalganbuki, it is no good for you.' But he didn't listen. Eventually the poison in his heart leaked deep into his spirit and the red mark became brighter.

'Keep away from that redback spider, Buki,' others would say. 'He's full of poison.'

The way they spoke about Budjari was the opposite. 'Whenever you need help, go and see that peacock spider, Budjari. He's such a good fulla.'

To this day, if you are lucky enough to see a peacock spider, it is very likely you will be drawn to him and your heart will be filled with happiness. And if you are lucky, he might even dance for you.

But when you see a redback spider, it is very likely you will want to run away, your heart filled with fear. This is a wise thing to do, because if you linger, he might try to bite you.

'Emily, you know how the little black snake story was your favourite?' Jacob said. 'I think this one is mine. In my mind, I could see Budjari hanging from his web like a trapeze artist.'

'I loved how the spiders started off looking the same but ended up looking different,' Emily added. 'I've never heard of a peacock spider.' She turned to her teacher. 'Ms Green, can we look up peacock spiders while we're in the library, please?'

'It's funny you should say that, Emily,' Ms Green replied. 'I'd never heard of them either. So, I looked them up. Here.' She held out her phone.

'They're so pretty,' Emily said. 'Just like in the story.'

'But they're so small,' Jacob said.

'Sometimes things are small in our stories to remind us to be humble,' Uncle Rolly said. 'Instead of getting angry when things didn't go right, Budjari was humble and learned from his mistakes.'

'And he never gave up, did he?' Jacob said. He looked at Emily. 'I felt like giving up on our

HAVING a YARN

presentation at the start, didn't I? But I'm looking forward to it now.'

'Staying positive when things are tough is important,' Uncle Rolly said. 'There were times when I felt like giving up on finding Carol, but I didn't. And now I'm keener than ever to find my brothers and their families.' The Elder pointed towards the big windows of the library. 'As you get older, there are going to be times when things aren't easy.'

Dark and menacing clouds glared. 'Storms can come into our lives just like they do in nature.'

'I don't like the sound of that,' Jacob said.

'Sometimes we can't avoid them,' Uncle Rolly continued. 'But the thing about storms is, they always pass.' He pointed out the window again. The clouds were disappearing. 'Our Old People teach us that storms can even be good for us. They teach us that hard times are a chance for us to learn.'

'That's what happened to Budjari, isn't it? Emily said. 'He learned from his hard times.'

'That's right. He had a goal, and he never gave up. But Budjari wasn't perfect, you know,' the uncle said. 'His brother gave him good advice sometimes, but Budjari didn't listen.' The screech of cockatoos carried into the library, and Uncle Rolly put his hand to his ear. 'Ah. Rain is on its way.'

'Did the birds tell you that?' Jacob blinked in disbelief.

'Yep. Plus, they said it was going to rain on the news this morning.' The room filled with the uncle's laughter. 'See, I use the old ways and the new ways.' He laughed even louder. 'You know the Old People have a saying: "If you come to me knowing everything, I can give you nothing. But if you come to me knowing nothing, I can give you everything." So, it's important to always be listening and learning, whether it be from nature, me, your parents, teachers, books or even the TV. Now ...' He put his hand in his pocket and brought out a small piece of paper. 'To help you get ready for your presentation, I thought I would give you a list of the main things I have talked about over the last little while.' He handed them the paper.

Ms Green looked at her watch. The children knew their last catch-up was about to finish, and Uncle Rolly was about to leave for the last time.

Ms Green stood up. 'Thank you so much, Uncle Rolly, for spending time with us. We've all learned so much.'

'Wait.' Jacob ran to a corner of the room and returned with a gift bag. Emily placed her card in it, then they handed Uncle Rolly their present.

He smiled and a tear ran down his cheek.

'I didn't expect this,' he said.

'Thank you,' Emily said.

'Thank you,' Jacob said.

'You are both part of my story now,' Uncle Rolly replied, 'and I'm very thankful for that.'

CONVERSATION POINT

What do you think was inside the gift bag?

What do you think was written in the card?

Why do you think it's important to be positive?

ACTIVITY

THINGS YOU WILL NEED:

- Coloured pencils, crayons or markers
- A blank sheet of paper.

Weathering Storms

Always remember that you don't have to face a storm on your own. It's okay to ask for help.

1. Imagine you're a tree on top of a hill. In the distance, you can see a huge storm coming towards you. It's tearing the forest apart. In a corner of your sheet of paper, draw a picture of how you are feeling.
2. Then you realise you aren't like the other trees. You are stronger and your roots go deep into the ground. Draw a picture of yourself as a tree, with lots of roots going into the ground.
3. All around the tree, write down what you need for your roots, trunk and branches to be strong.
   These could be things like:
   • knowing you are special • being grateful
   • not comparing yourself to others • being patient
   • caring for your body • loving yourself
   • being respectful, humble and kind • sharing
   • asking for help • good relationships • being positive.
4. You look at the storm again knowing that you are stronger than any other tree in the forest. In another corner of the page, draw a picture of how you are feeling now.
5. Are the two drawings of how you were feeling the same or different? If they are different, why are they different?

UNCLE ROLLY'S LIST

THESE ARE THE MAIN POINTS FROM THE STORIES, BUT THERE ARE MANY MORE.

WHAT ELSE WOULD YOU ADD TO THIS LIST?

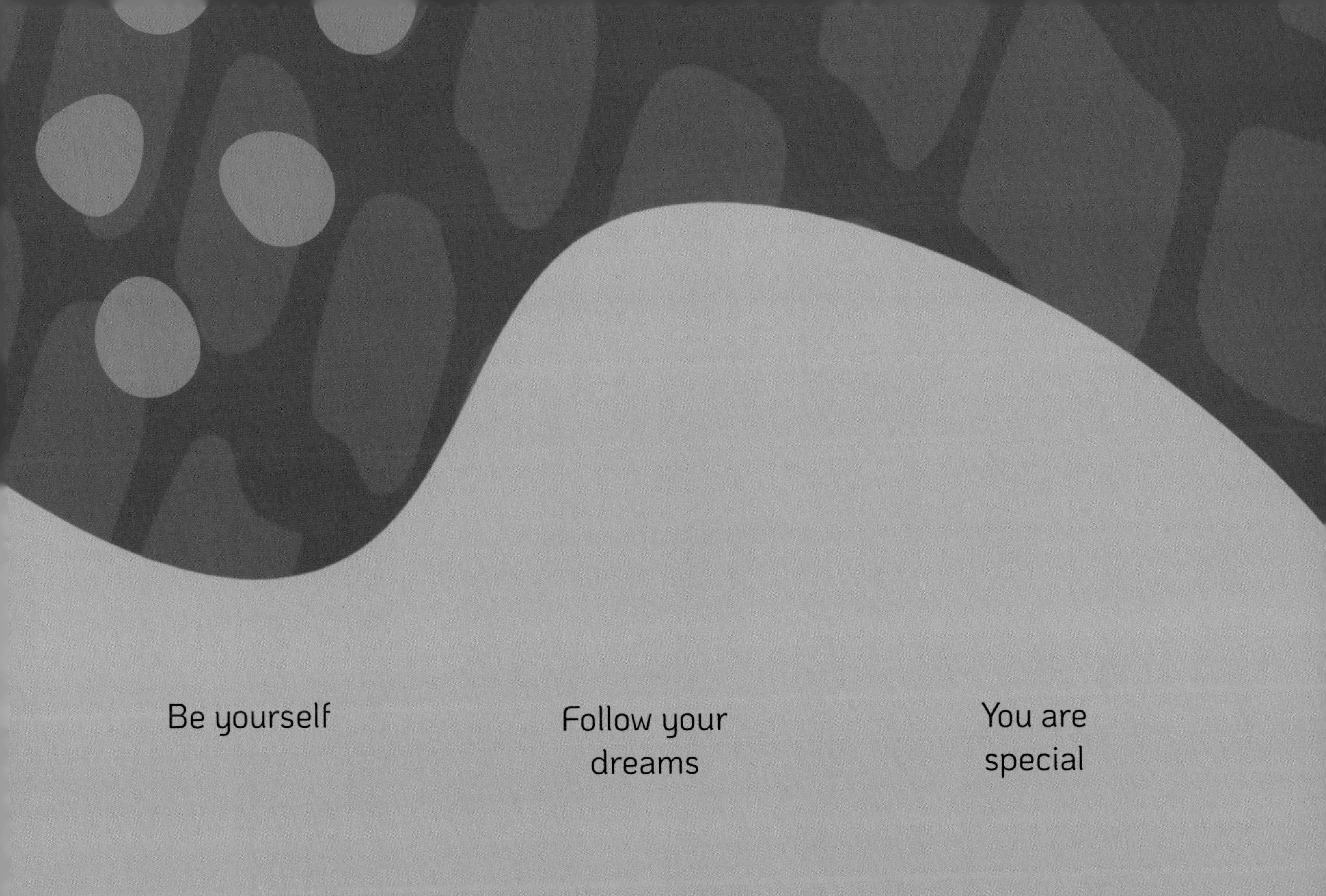

Be yourself

Follow your dreams

You are special

Love your body the way it is

If you are sad, take care of yourself

Do what you love but do it safely

Care for the land

You are never alone

Learn from your hard times

About the Illustrator

DYLAN FINNEY is an Australian-born Artist and Graphic Designer currently living on Darkinjung Land.

Whilst his dad was born in England, he is a proud descendant of the Marra, Ngalakgan and Yanyuwa clans in Arnhem Land on his mother's side. When not exploring the local bushland he's in the studio drawing or painting.

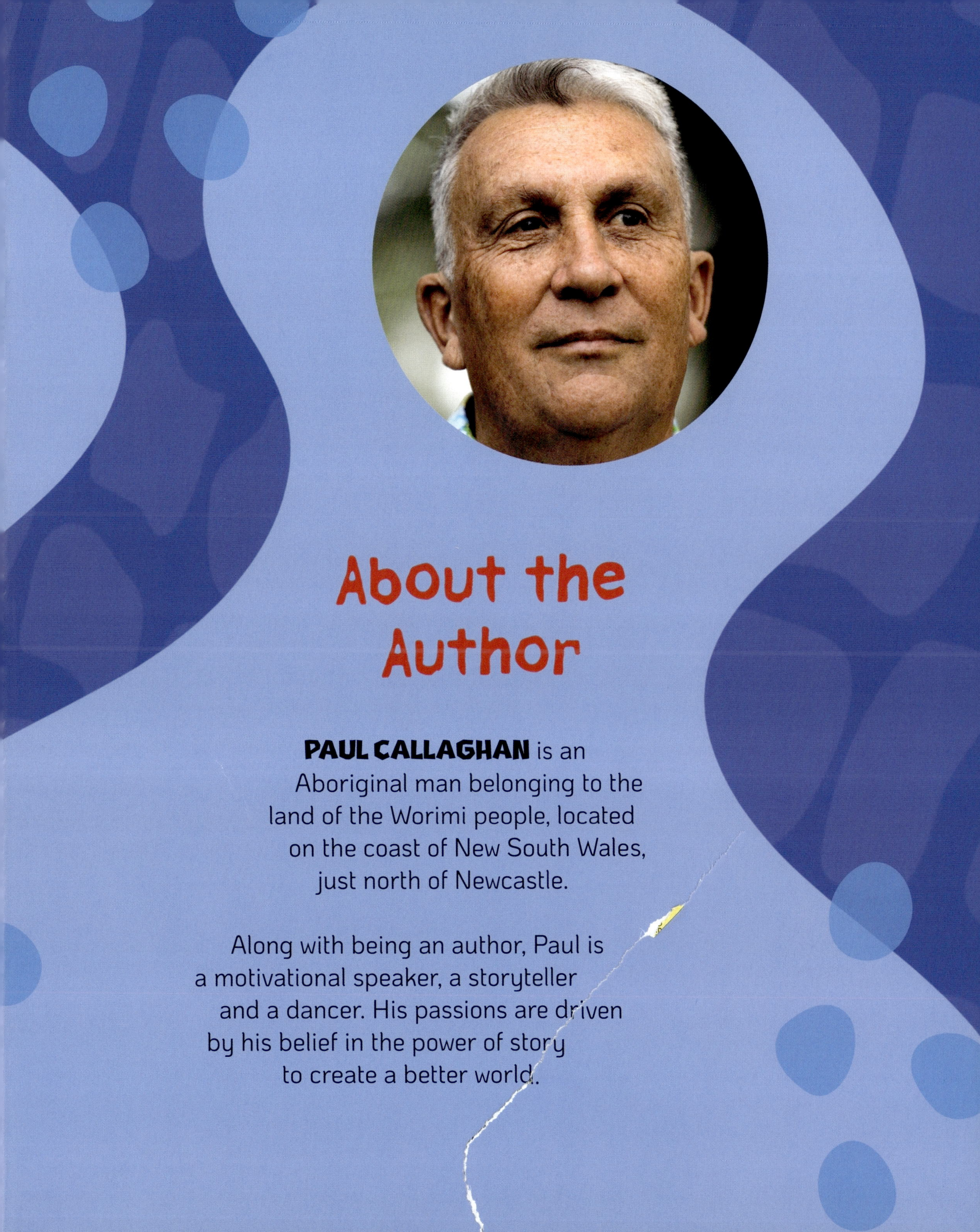

About the Author

PAUL CALLAGHAN is an Aboriginal man belonging to the land of the Worimi people, located on the coast of New South Wales, just north of Newcastle.

Along with being an author, Paul is a motivational speaker, a storyteller and a dancer. His passions are driven by his belief in the power of story to create a better world.

Pantera Press acknowledges the Aboriginal Traditional Custodians of Gadigal Country on which we work and pays respect to Elders both past and present.

First published in 2025 by Pantera Press, an imprint of Hardie Grant Publishing

Pantera Press
Gadigal Country
Level 7, 45 Jones Street
Ultimo NSW 2007

A Cataloguing-in-Publication entry for this work is available from the National Library of Australia.

ISBN 9780648748960 (Hardback)
ISBN 9781923390102 (eBook)

Cover design and internal illustrations: Dylan Finney
Publisher: Lex Hirst
Project editor: LinLi Wan
Editor: Lucy Bell
Proofreader: Kristina Schulz
Design and typesetting: Elysia Clapin
Author photo: Benjamin James Films

Printed in China by LEO Paper Products LTD

The paper this book is printed on is from FSC® certified forests and other controlled sources. FSC® promotes environmentally responsible, socially beneficial and economically viable management of the world's forests.